KNIT

4

SEASONS

KNIT 4 SEASONS

SUE CURL / ERIKA KNIGHT

Photography by
MICHAEL WOOLLEY

CHARLES SCRIBNER'S SONS   NEW YORK

Copyright © 1986 Sue Curl and Erika Knight

Library of Congress Cataloguing-in-Publication-Data

Curl, Sue.
    Knit 4 Seasons.

 Includes index.
 1. Knitting--Patterns.   I. Knight, Erika.
 II. Title.   III. Title: Knit 4 Seasons.
 TT825.C87   1986   746.9'2   86-21939
 ISBN 0-684-18791-4

First American Edition

Printed in West Germany by
Mohndruck Graphische Betriebe GmbH, Gütersloh

KNIT 4 SEASONS

SPRING

SUMMER

AUTUMN

WINTER

CONTENTS

KNITTING NOTES

TENSION OR GAUGE

Correct tension is the MOST IMPORTANT factor in making a successful garment. Often regarded as boring and unnecessary, even by the experienced knitter, a tension sample **must** be worked before beginning any pattern. Tension simply refers to the number of stitches and number of rows to each square centimetre of fabric.

TO MAKE A TENSION SAMPLE

1. Make a sample of at least 15cm square, using the yarn, needle size and stitch given in pattern.

2. Lay the sample on a smooth, flat surface (NEVER ON YOUR LAP), smooth out and allow to settle.

3. Place a pin in the centre of a stitch, about 3 stitches from edge; using a ruler measure 10cm from this pin, place 2nd pin in centre of stitch, count the number of stitches between pins, remembering that you begin with half a stitch and end with half a stitch (the stitches which are divided by the pins).

   A similar process will give you the number of rows.

4. Do not be tempted to cheat by stretching the sample; the original tension will have been calculated without stretching or pressing, unless specifically stated in the pattern.

5. If the number of stitches and rows does not correspond with the tension stated at the beginning of the pattern you must change your needle size.

6. If the number of stitches and rows is **more** than stated, try again on a **thinner** needle or your finished garment will be too large.

7. If the number of stitches and rows is **less** than stated, try again on a **thicker** needle or your finished garment will be too small.

8. Continue to try different needle sizes until the number of stitches and rows is the same as stated in the pattern.

9. Remember there is no such thing as an average tension. Patterns are made to the designer's tension; the knitter's tension must therefore correspond exactly to that of the designer.

10. Tension must be even, i.e. the same tension must be maintained throughout the work. The secret of working even tension is to let the yarn 'flow' smoothly through the fingers so that it forms even loops on the needles as the stitches are made.

Taking time at the beginning to check the tension saves time in the end. It ensures the finished garment accurately duplicates the look and intention of the designer and therefore avoids disappointment.

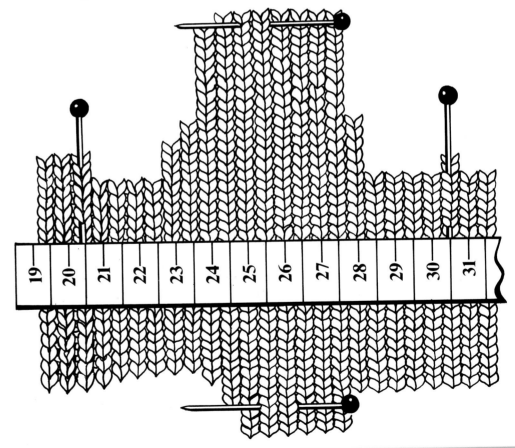

Please note that throughout this book all measurements are given in cm only. No attempt has been made to convert to inches as it is impossible to do so accurately.

YARN SUBSTITUTION

We recommend that you use the yarn specified in your pattern. This will give you the best results and allow you to match exactly the look and texture of the design.

If, however, you are unable to purchase the yarn specified, remember the following tips:

1. The most important factor in yarn substitution is matching the tension required by the pattern. ALWAYS CHECK YOUR TENSION CAREFULLY.

2. You should always use the **type** of yarn used in the pattern – for example, always use mohair if the pattern calls for a mohair or a boucle if it calls for a boucle, etc.

   The texture of a yarn is a major factor in determining tension and it is very difficult to substitute one texture for another successfully.

3. Be sure you have enough yarn to complete the garment, as the number of metres on each ball of the substitute yarn may be different from the original.

KNITTING NEEDLES

US	METRIC	UK
0	2mm	14
1	2¼mm	13
	2½mm	
2	2¾mm	12
	3mm	11
3	3¼mm	10
4	3½mm	
5	3¾mm	9
	4mm	8
6		
7	4½mm	7
8	5mm	6
9	5½mm	5
10	6mm	4
10½	6½mm	3
	7mm	2
	7½mm	1
11	8mm	0
13	9mm	00
15	10mm	000

To avoid any confusion the needle sizes are given only in millimetres (mm) in the text itself.

GRADES Each pattern has been given a grade to specify at a glance the knitting standard required to make the garment.

 for the beginner – basic stitches, requiring little shaping and simple finishing.

 for the knitter with a little experience – more complex stitches, but still with little shaping and simple finishing.

 for the more experienced knitter – requiring more skills, including more complexity in shaping and finishing.

TERMS

cap shaped top of sleeve

cast off close the knitting loops by lifting the first st over the 2nd, the 2nd over the 3rd, etc. (US bind off)

cast off in rib cast off the sts whilst working the cast-off row in rib (US bind off in rib)

continue (or work) straight continue knitting in the specified pattern without increasing or decreasing (US work even)

increase add to the number of sts in a row by working 2 sts in 1 st, i.e. k into front and back of st

decrease reduce the number of sts in a row by working 2 sts together

knitwise insert the needle into the st as if you were about to knit it

make one add to the number of sts in a row by inserting the right-hand needle from front to back under horizontal strand between the last st worked and next stitch on left needle, forming loop over left needle, knit through back loop of this st

pick up and knit (purl) knit (or purl) into the loops along the edge of fabric

purlwise insert the needle into the stitch as if you were about to purl it

reverse stocking st purl all right-side rows and knit all wrong-side rows, for circular knitting purl all rounds (US reverse stockinette stitch)

selvedge stitch edge stitch used for neater finishing

slip stitch in knitting this term refers to a stitch which is passed from the needle without being worked

stocking stitch knit all the right-side rows and purl all the wrong-side rows; in circular knitting knit all rounds (US stockinette stitch)

yarn over in knitting this term refers to making a new stitch by looping the yarn over the needle, also yfwd, yo, yrn

ABBREVIATIONS

alt	alternate
approx	approximately
beg	beginning
C	contrasting colour
cm	centimetre(s)
cn	cable needle
cont	continu(e)(ing)
dec	decreas(e)(ing)
dpn	double-pointed needles
foll	follow(s)(ing)
g st	garter stitch
grp(s)	group(s)
inc	increas(e)(ing)
k	knit
kb	knit into back of stitch
kwise	knitwise
MC	main colour
m1	make 1
mm	millimetres
p	purl
patt(s)	pattern(s)
psso	pass slip stitch(es) over
pwise	purlwise
rem	remain(s)(ing)
rep	repeat
rev st st	reverse stocking stitch (reverse stockinette stitch)
rib	ribbing
RH	right hand
RS	right side(s)
SKP	slip 1, k 1, pass slip stitch(es) over
sl	slip
sl st	slip stitch
st(s)	stitch(es)
st st	stocking stitch (stockinette stitch)
tbl	through back loop
tog	together
WS	wrong side
wyib	with yarn in back of work
wyif	with yarn in front of work
yb	yarn back
yfwd	yarn forward
yo	yarn over
yrn	yarn round needle
*	repeat directions following * as many times as indicated
( )	repeat directions inside brackets as many times as indicated

KNITTING NOTES

Reading Patterns

Always read the pattern through very carefully before starting work.

Grades and Sizes

Each pattern gives both a chest size and a finished measurement. The amount of ease has been calculated for each individual design to create a particular look and may vary from pattern to pattern.

Working from charts

Colour patterns are often worked from charts and the colours are indicated by symbols.

Each square represents a stitch and each row of squares represents a row of knitting.

The patterns are worked in stocking stitch, i.e. one row knit, one row purl, unless otherwise stated.

Read the knit rows from right to left and read the purl rows from left to right (unless otherwise instructed by the pattern).

Continue to work on this principle until the design is completed.

Colour Knitting

There are 2 popular methods of working in colours.

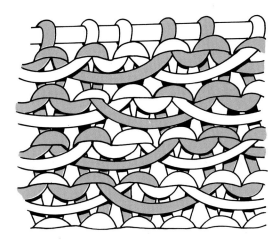

Stranding or Fair Isle – work with each colour, according to the sequence from the chart, letting the colour not in use drop and strand itself loosely across the back of the fabric.

Swiss Darning or Duplicate Stitch

This is a very simple method of applying coloured patterns to a finished garment, especially where there are single coloured stitches, widely spaced, which makes knitting them impractical.

The embroidered stitch is worked on top of the knitted stitches in a contrast colour.

Using a blunt end or crewel needle and the colour required in a yarn of a similar weight, darn the yarn invisibly at the back, *bring the needle up through centre of stitch from the back of the work, insert the needle from right to left, behind the stitch immediately above.

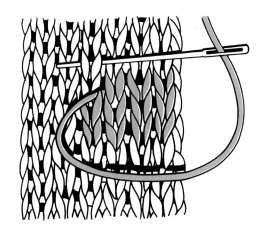

Place needle down centre of original stitch and out through the centre of st to left, repeat from *

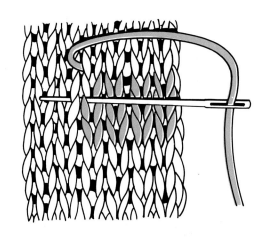

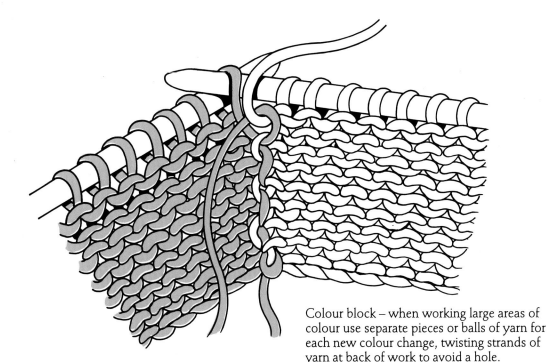

Colour block – when working large areas of colour use separate pieces or balls of yarn for each new colour change, twisting strands of yarn at back of work to avoid a hole.

TIPS FOR THE PROFESSIONAL FINISH

Check the pattern before finishing, it will list which techniques are appropriate to each garment and the order to work in.

1. Picking Up Stitches

To pick up stitches evenly, divide edge into regular sections with pins placed at right angles to edge, then divide total number of stitches required by the number of sections, pick up that number of stitches between each pin.

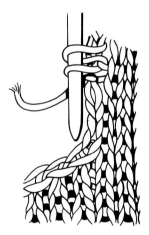

2. Ends

Sew in ends, using a blunt needle 'weave' each end separately across the fabric of the work on the wrong side (never along the edges) for about 4 stitches, then back 1 or 2 stitches to hold end firmly in place.

3. Block and Pin

To block a piece of knitting pin it out to the correct size and shape on a padded surface (a table covered with a folded blanket under a sheet is ideal). Pin each piece, wrong side facing up. Do not stretch or distort the fabric. Make sure all the rows run in straight lines. Check that the width and length of each piece match the measurements given on the pattern. Pin closely around the edge of each piece of knitting, placing pins at right angles to the edges.

4. Steam

Set iron to steam setting, hold the iron above work, allowing the steam to penetrate the whole of the fabric. Leave to settle until cool with the pins still in place.

5. Press

Place a clean damp cloth over the knitting, press the work by placing the iron on to the fabric, lift the iron in the air, then place it down on the next part of the fabric until the whole piece is pressed. Remove the cloth, leave to settle until dry with the pins still in place. Never 'iron' knitting. i.e. run iron to and fro over the fabric, as this will distort the work.

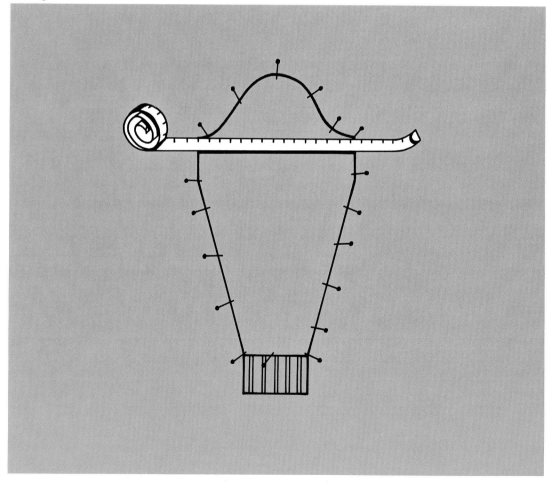

KNITTING NOTES

TIPS FOR THE PROFESSIONAL FINISH

6. Seams

(a) Invisible Seam, used to join all side and sleeve seams, or where a flat seam with no bulk is required.

With right side of both pieces facing secure the yarn to edge of one piece. Take the needle across to the opposite edge, pick up the equivalent stitch on this piece, pull the yarn through; take the needle back to first edge, returning the needle through hole of previous stitch, picking up the next stitch pull the yarn through.

Continue in this way picking up and pulling together stitch to stitch (row for row) along length of seam.

(b) Back Stitch Seam, used where a firm edge is required to hold the shape, such as a set-in sleeve, or to give strength at any point where the garment may take extra strain. Can also be used as a decorative feature of the design.

Place the pieces together, right side facing rightside. Work along wrong side of the fabric one stitch from the edge.

Secure the yarn and work from right to left. With the needle at back of work move along to the left, the length of one knitted stitch, bring the needle through fabric to front, pull the yarn through, take the needle from left to right across front of work, to end of the last stitch, put the needle through fabric to back of work, pull the yarn through.

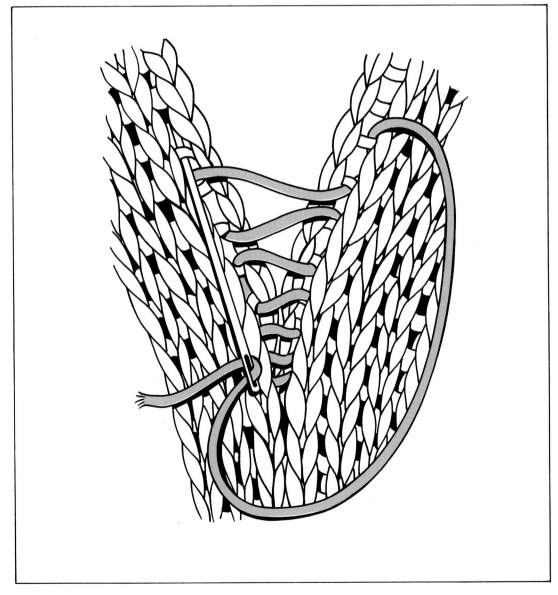

(c) Slip Stitch

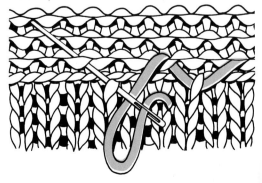

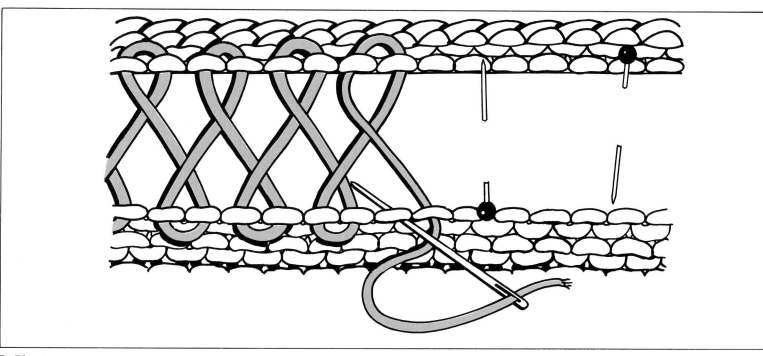

7. Elastic

Cut the elastic to fit waist, allowing 4cm extra. Make a seam by overlapping the edges and oversewing.

Place elastic round the waist on the wrong side.

1) With a herringbone stitch make a casing over the elastic

2) Fold hem over the elastic, stitch into place.

8. Zips

Pin the zip to the opening, being sure that the knitting fits easily and is not wrinkled or stretched. The knitted edges should come right up to the teeth of the zip. Work in back stitch along the edges using sewing thread. Be sure to choose a zip that is the correct weight for the garment.

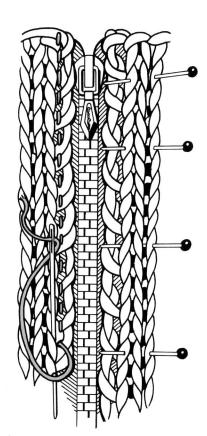

9. Teasing

To tease or brush finished garments in mohair or brushed yarns.

10. Shoulder Pads

An important part of the design, in unstructured garments a pad gives the shoulders added softness and depth. In cardigans, jackets and more tailored garments pads create a dramatic silhouette.

(a) Set in Sleeve

Place centre of pad along shoulder seam, and folded edge to armhole edge, carefully sew in place using a slip stitch. Secure pointed end to shoulder seam.

(b) Drop Shoulders

Position the pad to suit you, pin into place. Carefully sew centre of pad to shoulder seam.

> **"Oh, to be in England,
> Now that April's there."**
> *Robert Browning*

SPRING

Lace and cable stitches
give scalloped detail to long 20's top

Beads and Embroidery

Try Black/Grey white & red
as alternative colour combination

SPRING

DESIGN NUMBER 1
'COLLEGE CARDIGAN' – Erika

THE PATTERNS

Description

Loose, drop shoulder, 'V' neck cardigan worked in stripe pattern, with 'heraldic' motifs, 5 buttons and pocket details.

Materials

Jaegar 'Monte Cristo'

A – Blue 6(7) × 50 gram balls

B – Jade 7(7) × 50 gram balls

C – White 3(3) × 50 gram balls

One pair each needles 3¼mm and 4mm and stitch holder

5 white buttons

Measurements

To fit chest
92–102cm   102–112cm

Actual measurements
117cm   127cm

Length from shoulder
70cm   74cm

Sleeve seam
48cm   51cm

Tension

22 sts and 26 rows to 10cm sq measured over st st on 4mm needles.

NB Pattern uses colour block technique and chart.

BACK

With 3¼mm needles and C cast on 122(130) sts and work in k1 p1 rib for 2 rows.
Change to A and rib until work measures 8cm.

Inc row: Rib 12(13), * inc into next st, rib 13(12), rep from * to last 12(13) sts, inc into next st, rib to end [130(139) sts].

Change to 4mm needles and stocking stitch and using colour block method set stripe pattern as follows:

Row 1: * k14(15) B, k1(1) C, k14(15) A, rep from * to last 14(15) sts, k14(15) B.
Keeping continuity of stripes work in st st until work measures 20(21.5)cm from cast-on edge.
Work 2 rows in C only.
Change to B and st st for 4 rows.

Now set pattern for shields as follows:-
k26(29) B, [1C, 1A, (start of shield 1)], k36(38) B, [2A(start of shield 2)] k36(38) B, [2C, (start of shield 3)], k26(28) B.

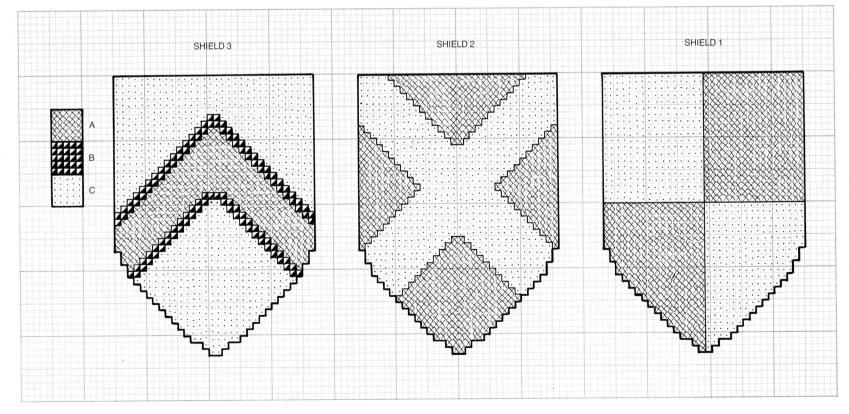

SHIELD 3   SHIELD 2   SHIELD 1

A

B

C

Continue in st st working shields in colours as indicated on chart with B as main background colour.
When shields are complete work 5 rows in B only, then 2 rows in C only.
When work measures 41(43)cm from cast-on edge place coloured markers at each end of row to indicate armhole position.
Next set colours for stripe sequence as on Row 1 and continue until work measures 67(71)cm from cast-on edge.

Shape shoulders by casting off 15(16) sts at beg of next 4 rows, then 16(17) sts at beg of next 2 rows. Work 1 row.
Cast off remaining sts.

Pocket Linings

Right front – With 4mm needles and A cast on 28(30) sts and with RS facing k14(15) A, k14(15) B.
Work in st st as set until work measures 13(14)cm, leave sts on a holder.
Left front – Work as for right but reverse the colours, i.e. k14(15) B, k14(15) A.

RIGHT FRONT

*** With 3¼mm needles and C cast on 54(58) sts and k1 p1 rib for 2 rows.
Change to A and rib until work measures 8cm.
Inc. row: * rib 10(11), inc. into next st, rep from * 4 times, rib to end, 58(62) sts ***
Change to 4mm needles and st st and set stripe sequence as follows:-
* k14(15) B, k1(1) C, k14(15) A *, rep from * to *
Continue as set in st st until work measures 18(19)cm.
Place pocket top as follows:-
Next row: k14(15) B, k1(1) C, k1 p1 rib in A for 28(30) sts, k1(1) C, k14(15) A.
Continue with centre sts in rib until 2.5cm has been worked in rib.
Next row: p14(15) A, p1(1) C, cast off 28(30) in rib, p1(1) C, p14(15) B.
Now work 2 rows in C placing pocket lining in place of those cast off in previous row.
Change to B and work 4 rows.
Place shield no. 3 as follows:-
k30(32) B, k2 C, k26(28) B.
Continue to work shield and then the other colour sequences to match back.
When work measures 37(39)cm shape neck as follows:-
Dec 1 st at neck edge on foll 3 alt rows, then 1 st at neck edge on foll 4th rows 5 times, then on foll 8th rows until 46(49) sts remain.
At the same time when work measures 41(43) cm from cast-on edge place a coloured marker at side edge to indicate armhole position.

Continue straight in stripe sequence until front is same length as back and cast off shoulder to match back.

LEFT FRONT

Work rib and increases as for right front (from *** to ***).
Change to 4mm needles and set pattern as follows:
* k14(15) A, k1(1) C, k14(15) B *, rep from * to *
Continue as for right front placing pocket as before.
Place shield no. 2 as follows:
k26(28) B, k2 A, k30(32) B.
Now complete to match other front reversing neck shaping.

SLEEVES (2 alike)

With 3¼mm needles and C cast on 60(64) sts and k1 p1 for 2 rows.
Change to A and rib until work measures 8cm.

Inc row: Rib 7(9), * inc into next st, rib 8, rep from * to last 8(10) sts, inc into next st, rib to end [66(70) sts].
Change to 4mm needles and st st and set pattern as follows:
k4(4) B, * k1(1) C, k14(15) A, k14(15) B *, rep from * to *, k1(1) C, k3(3) A.
Work in stripe sequence as set for the whole sleeve, AT THE SAME TIME increasing 1 st at each end of every 4th row until 116(124) sts are being worked, taking the extra sts into the stripe pattern.
Continue straight until work measures 48(51)cm. Cast off.

BUTTONBAND

Refer to 'Tips for the Professional Finish'.
Join shoulder seam, with an invisible seam.
With 3¼mm needles and A pick up approx 170 sts evenly up right front and round 'V' neck to finish at centre back.
Work in k1 p1 rib for 5cm.
Change to A and rib for 2 rows. Cast off. ribwise.

BUTTONHOLE BAND

Pick up as for right front and rib for 2.5cm.
Place 5 buttonholes by casting off 3 sts for each buttonhole and casting on over them in the next row. Place first buttonhole about 2.5cm from the bottom and then four more at intervals of approx 9(10)cm, with the fifth buttonhole just below start of neck shaping.
Complete to match other front.

TO MAKE UP

Refer to 'Tips for the Professional Finish'.
1) Weave in all ends.
2) Block and pin and steam.
3) Lay work out flat and set in sleeves, using an invisible seam, between coloured markers.
4) With an invisible seam sew sleeve seam and side seams.
5) Sew pocket linings to inside of fronts with slip stitch.
6) Sew on buttons.

SPRING

Description

Long cardigan, with oversize 'V' neck, worked in bold stripe pattern with badge motif and pocket details.

Materials

Jaeger Monte Cristo

A – White 12 × 50 gram balls

B – Jade 7 × 50 gram balls

C – Blue 2 × 50 gram balls

D – Pale Blue 2× 50 gram balls

One pair each needles sizes 4mm and 3¼mm

3 large buttons

Measurements

One size

Actual measurement
127cm

Length from shoulder
99cm

Sleeve seam (approx)
46cm

Tension

22 sts and 24 rows to 10cm sq measured over st st on 4mm needles.

NB Pattern uses colour block method

BACK

Using 3¼mm needles and B cast on 145 sts and work in k1 p1 rib for 2 rows.
Change to A and continue in rib until work measures 8cm.
Change to 4mm needles and st st and place stripe pattern as follows using colour block method.
* k15 B, k2 C, k15 A, rep from * 3 times more, k15 B, k2 C.
Continue in st st as now set until work measures 65cm from cast-on edge.
Place coloured threads at each end of row to indicate armhole positions.
Continue in stripe sequence until work measures 97cm.
Shape shoulders by casting off 16 sts at beg of next 2 rows, then 17 sts at beg of next 4 rows.
Work 1 row then cast off remaining 45 sts.

POCKET LININGS

Left Front

With A and 4mm needles cast on 34 sts and work in st st setting pattern as follows: K2 C, k15 B, k15 A, k2 C.
Work in stripe sequence as now set for 18cm, leaving sts on a spare needle.

Right Front

Work as for left setting stripes as follows:
k2 C, k15 A, k15 B, k2 C.

LEFT FRONT

With 3¼mm needles and B cast on 64 sts and work in k1 p1 rib for 2 rows.
Change to A and rib until work measures 8cm.
Change to 4mm needles and working in colour block set stripes as follows: k15 A, k2 C, k15 B, K15 A, k2 C, k15 B.
Work in st st in stripes as set until work measures 27cm.
Place pocket top as follows with right side facing:
K15 A, work next 34 sts in k1 p1 rib in A, k15 B.
Continue as set until 7 rows of rib for pocket top have been worked.
Next row: P15 B, rib 34 sts in B, p15 A.
Next row: K15 A, cast off 34 sts in B in rib, k15 B.
Cont in st st and stripe sequence placing sts from pocket lining in place of those cast off in previous row and work straight until work

measures 46cm from cast-on edge.
Shape neck by dec 1 st at neck edge on next 2 rows, then dec 1 st at neck edge of next alt row, then on foll 4th rows 4 times, on foll 6th rows 4 times, then on foll 8th rows until 50 sts remain.
At the same time when there are 60 sts on needle start motif approx 30 rows above pocket as follows:
K15 A, k2 C, k12 B, **k2 D, k2 B, k1 A, k2 D,** k12 A, k2 C, k11 B.
Continue in stripe sequence working badge motif from diagram.
Continue straight on 50 sts until work measures 97cm and work shoulder shapings to match back.

RIGHT FRONT

Work as for left front but place stripe sequence as follows:
K15 B, k2 C, k15 A, k15 B, k2 C, k15 A.
Complete to match left front reversing all shapings and omitting badge motif.

SLEEVES (2 alike)

With 3¼mm needles and B cast on 82 sts and work k1 p1 rib for 2 rows.
Change to A and rib until work measures 8cm.
Change to 4mm needles and st st and set stripe sequence as follows:
K8 B, * k2 C, k15 A, k15 B, rep from * once, k2 C, k8 A.
Continue in stripes as now set, AT THE SAME TIME inc 1 st at each end of every foll 3rd row until 138 sts are reached, working extra sts into stripe pattern.
Continue straight until work measures 46cm.
Cast off.

BUTTONBAND

Refer to 'Tips for the Professional Finish'.
Join shoulder seams with an invisible stitch.
Using 3¼mm needles and A pick up 130 sts from bottom rib to neck shaping and a further 140 sts up round V neck and 20 sts to centre back of neck.
Work in k1 p1 rib for 15 rows.
Change to B and rib 1 row, then cast off in rib in B.

KNITTING STANDARD ✕ ✕ ✕

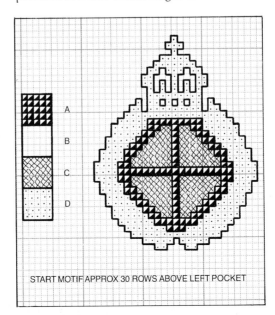

START MOTIF APPROX 30 ROWS ABOVE LEFT POCKET

BUTTONHOLE BAND

Work as for other band for 8 rows.
Row 9: (from bottom edge) Rib 8, cast off 7 sts, rib 50, cast off 7 sts, rib 50, cast off 7 sts, rib to end of row.
Row 10: Rib, casting on 7 sts over those cast off in previous row.
Work a further 5 rows rib in A, then work 1 row in B and cast off rib in B.

TO MAKE UP

Refer to 'Tips for the Professional Finish'.

1) Weave in all ends.
2) Block and Pin.
3) Press, omitting all ribbing.
4) Open work out flat and set in sleeves between armhole markers with 'Invisible Stitch'.
5) With back stitch sew sleeve seams.
6) With invisible stitch sew side seams.
7) Slip stitch pocket linings down on inside of work.
8) Sew on buttons.

'KNITTED SHIRT'

KNITTING STANDARD ✕

Description

Long-sleeved, loose, easy-fitting sports shirt in choice of cotton or wool.

Materials

Spring – Neveda Cotton 4 ply 9(9:10) × 50 gram balls or
Autumn – Patons Diploma 4 ply 8(8:9) × 50 gram balls.

One pair each needles sizes 3¼mm and 2¼mm and 2¾mm and spare needle.

3 buttons

Measurements

To fit bust
81–86cm   91–97cm   102–107cm

Actual measurements
105cm   109cm   114cm

Length from shoulder
67cm   70cm   72cm

Sleeve seam
47cm   48cm   51cm

Tension

26 sts and 32 rows to 10cm sq measured over st st on 3¼mm needles.

BACK

* Using 2¾mm needles cast on 126(132:138) sts and work in k1 p1 rib for 8cm.
Inc row: Rib 8(11:10), * inc into next st, rib 11(11:12), rep from * to last 10(13:10) sts, inc into next st, rib to end [136(142:148)].
Change to 3¼mm needles and st st and work until back measures 41(42:43)cm from cast-on edge. ***
Mark each end of next row with coloured thread to indicate armholes.
Continue straight in st st until work measures 66(69:71)cm from cast-on edge, ending with a purl row.

Shape shoulders by casting off as follows:
Cast off 15(16:17) sts at beg of next 2 rows, 16(16:17) sts at beg of next 2 rows and 16(17:17) sts at beg of next 2 rows.
Work 1 row then cast off remaining 42(44:46) sts.

POCKET LINING

With 3¼mm needles cast on 32 sts and work in st st for 13cm, ending with a purl row, leave sts on a spare needle.

FRONT

Work as for back from * to ***, ending with a knit row.
Place coloured threads at each side of work to indicate armholes.
Next row: P85(89:93), p next 32 sts and leave on a holder, purl to end.
Next row: K19(21:23), k32 sts from pocket lining, k to end of row.
Work in st st until work measures 43(44:46)cm, ending with a purl row.
Divide for front opening as follows:
Next row: K63(66:69) sts, cast off centre 10 sts, knit to end of row.
Work on each set of sts separately.

Left Front

Cont straight until work measures 60(61:64)cm ending with a purl row.
Cast off 6(7:8) sts at neck edge on next row, then cast off 2 sts at neck edge on next alt row, then dec 1 st at neck edge on next 5 rows, then dec 1 st at neck edge on next 3 alt rows [47(49:51) sts].
Continue straight until front is same length as back and cast off shoulders to match back.

Right Front

Complete to match, reversing all shapings.

SLEEVES (2 alike)

With 2¾mm needles cast on 62(68:74) sts and work in k1 p1 rib for 8cm.
Inc row: Rib 4(6:8), *inc into next st, rib 5, rep from * to last 4(8:12) sts inc into next st, rib to end [72(78:84) sts].
Change to 3¼mm needles and st st and work, inc 1 st at each end of next and every foll 4th row until 130(136:144) sts are reached.
Work straight until work measures 47(48:51)cm. Cast off.

BUTTON BAND

(Right front band for man)
(Left front band for woman)
With 2¾mm needles and RS facing pick up 53(58:64) sts down right front.
Row 1: K1, *k1, p1, rep from * to last st, k1.
Row 2: K2, *p1, k1, rep from * to end.
Repeat these 2 rows for 12 rows. Cast off firmly in rib.

BUTTONHOLE BAND

(Left front band for man)
(Right front band for woman)
Pick up and work as for right front for 5 rows.
Row 6: Rib 7, *cast off 3 sts, rib 14(17:20) sts, rep from * once, cast off 3 sts, rib 8.
Row 7: Rib, casting on 3 sts in place of those cast off on previous row.
Rib for a further 5 rows. Cast off firmly in rib.

POCKET TOP

With 2¾mm needles and RS facing pick up 32 sts from st holder and work in k1 p1 rib for 4cm. Cast off evenly in rib.

COLLAR

With 2¼mm needles cast on 199(203:205) sts.
Row 1: K2, * p1, k1, rep from * to last st, k1.
Row 2: * K1, p1, rep from * to last st, k1
Repeat these 2 rows for 5cm.
Change to 2¾mm needles and work for a further 5cm.
Cast off firmly in rib.

TO MAKE UP

Refer to 'Tips for the Professional Finish'.

1) Weave in all ends.
2) Block and pin.
3) Press, omitting all ribbing.
4) With invisible seam sew shoulders.
5) Lay work out flat and set in sleeves between armhole markers with an invisible seam.
6) With an invisible seam sew sleeve and side seams.
7) Turn work to inside and slip stitch pocket lining into position on RS of work.
8) Slip stitch buttonhole band over button band into position; and sew on buttons.
9) Sew on collar – fold collar in half to find centre, and pin this point to centre back.
10) Slip stitch into position, working towards front on either side.

'FINE LEGGING'

KNITTING STANDARD ✕

Description

Easy-fitting leggings in fine cotton with elastic waistband.

Materials

Knitting Fever 4 ply cotton 6 × 50gram balls.

One pair each needles sizes 3¼mm and 2¾mm

Elastic (6cm wide) to fit waist.

Measurements
One Size

Leg seam: 61cm.

Tension

32 sts and 40 rows to 10cm square measured over st st on 3¼mm needles.

LEFT LEG

With 2¾mm needles cast on 70 sts and work in k1 p1 rib for 13cm.

Change to 3¼mm needles and work in stocking stitch.

Inc 1 st at each end of every 4th row until 88 sts are reached.

Work without further shaping for 13cm.

Now inc 1 st at each end of next and every foll 4th row until 144 sts are reached.

Mark each end of last row with a coloured thread to indicate top of leg seam ***

Work 53 rows without shaping.

Next row: (WS facing) p2 tog, p to end of row.

Dec this way on every foll 4th row until 133 sts remain.

Shape for back as follows:

Row 1:   K1, k2 tog, k56 , TURN.
Row 2 and alt rows: Purl.
Row 3:   k54, TURN.
Row 5:   K1, k2 tog, k47, TURN.
Row 7:   K45, TURN.
Row 9:   K1, k2 tog, k38, TURN.
Row 11: K36, TURN.

Continue without further shaping at beg of row but working 4 sts less on each knit row until down to 8 sts, ending with purl row.

Change to 2¾mm needles and work in k1 p1 rib for 60 rows.

Cast off.

RIGHT LEG

Work as for left leg to ***

Work 52 rows without shaping.

Next row: (RS facing) k2 tog, k to end.

Dec in this way every foll 4th row until 133 sts remain.

Dec for back as for left leg but on purl row, i.e.

Row 1: P1, p2 tog, p56, TURN.
Row 2 and alt rows: Knit.

Complete to match left leg.

GUSSET

With 3¼mm needles cast on 2 sts and working in st st inc 1 st at each end of every alt row until 20 sts are reached, then dec back down to 2 sts.

Cast off.

TO MAKE UP

Refer to 'Tips for the Professional Finish'.

1) Weave in all ends.
2) Block and pin and press, omitting ribbing.
3) Sew leg seams to markers with back stitch.
4) With invisible stitch sew back and front seams to gusset and sew gusset neatly between leg seams.
5) Referring to 'Tips for the Professional Finish' sew elastic in waistband, using second method.

Description

Long 20's top with button front in 'lace and cables'.

MATERIALS

Richard Poppleton Firenza 12(14) × 50 gram balls

One pair each needles sizes 4mm and 3¼mm, 1 cable needle

2 mother of pearl buttons.

Measurements

To fit bust
81–86cm   91–106cm

Actual measurements
98cm   112cm

Length from shoulder
72cm   74cm

Sleeve seam (approx)
30cm   30cm

Additional Abbreviation

Cr6 = sl 3 sts onto cn, hold at front of work, k3, k sts on cn.

Tension

26 sts and 28 rows to 10cm sq measured over the patt on size 4mm needles.

BACK

With 3¼mm needles, cast on 128(146) sts fairly loosely.
K4 rows.
Cont in patt as follows.
1st row: (WS) K1, p to last st, k1.
2nd row: K1, (k2 tog) 3 times, * (yfwd, k1) 6 times, (k2 tog) 6 times; rep from * to last 13 sts, (yfwd, k1) 6 times, (k2 tog) 3 times, k1.
3rd row: K1, p3, * k12, p6; rep from * to last 16 sts, k12, p3, k1.
4th row: K16, * Cr6, k12; rep from * to last 4 sts, k4.
5th to 7th rows: As 1st to 3rd rows.
8th row: K to end.

These 8 rows form the patt.
Rep these 8 rows 4 times more.
Change to 4mm needles.
Cont in patt until work measures 43(45)cm from cast-on edge, along side edge. Mark side edges with a contrast thread, to indicate beg of armhole. **

Work a further 27cm in patt, ending with either the 2nd or 6th row of patt.
K3 rows. Cast off.

FRONT

Work as for Back to **
Work a further 11cm in patt, ending with a WS row.

Divide Front

While keeping patt correct, patt 58(67) sts and leave them on a spare needle, cast off the next 12 sts, patt to end.
Cont in patt on the last set of sts until Front measures 27cm from marker thread, ending with either the 2nd or 6th row of patt.
K3 rows. Cast off.
With WS of work facing, rejoin yarn to sts on spare needle and complete to match opposite side.

SLEEVES (both alike, both sizes)

With 3¼mm needles, cast on 146 sts fairly loosely and k4 rows, then rep the 8 patt rows as given for Back 3 times.

Change to 4mm needles.
Cont in patt until Sleeve measures 30cm, ending with a WS row.
Cast off.

BUTTONHOLE BAND

With RS facing and using 3¼mm needles, pick up and k29 sts, evenly along right front edge of neck opening.
1st row: K1, * p1, k1; rep from * to end.
2nd row: P1, * k1, p1; rep from * to end.

Rep these 2 rows twice more, then the 1st row again.
1st buttonhole row: Rib 5, cast off the next 2 sts, rib 15 including st used in casting off, cast off the next 2 sts, rib to end.
2nd buttonhole row: Rib 5, cast on 2, rib 15, cast on 2, rib 5.

Work 7 more rows in rib.
Cast off ribwise.

BUTTON BAND

With RS facing and using 3¼mm needles, pick up and k29 sts along left front edge of neck opening. Work 16 rows in rib. Cast off ribwise.

SHOULDER PADS (make 2)

With 3¼mm needles, cast on 39 sts.
Work a square in rib as given for buttonhole band.
Cast off ribwise.

TO COMPLETE

Check the techniques used in 'Tips for the Professional Finish'.

1) Weave in ends.
2) Block and pin.
3) Steam.
4) With invisible seams, sew front bands to the cast-off stitches of neck opening, right overlapping left. Join shoulders for 14(17)cm from side edges. Join sides to marker threads. Join sleeves.
5) With a back stitch, set in sleeves.
6) Sew shoulder pads in place.
7) Sew buttons on to left front band.

SPRING

'TEACHER'S PET' – Sue

Description

Soft Angora jumper with beaded and embroidered flowers.

Materials

Jaeger Angora Spun MC – 9(10:11:12) × 20 gram balls
Jaegar Alpaca C – 1(1:1:1) × 50 gram ball
Odd ball of DK in toning colour for embroidery

270 beads ref. PB3 col. 22 from Ells and Farrier

One pair each of 3¼mm and 2¾mm knitting needles.

Measurements

To fit bust

81cm	86cm	91cm	96cm

Actual measurements

88cm	93·5cm	99cm	105cm

Length from shoulder

60cm	60cm	60cm	60cm

Sleeve seam (approx)

40cm	40cm	40cm	40cm

Additional Abbreviations

B1 = bead 1, take yarn to RS of work, sl next st, push bead close to work letting it lie on top of sl st, return yarn to WS; MB = make bobble, (k1,p1) twice in next st, turn, p4, turn, k4, turn, p2 tog twice, turn, k2 tog; C = contrast yarn.

Tension

28 sts and 36 rows to 10cm sq measured over st st on size 3¼mm needles.

BACK AND FRONT ALIKE

With 2¾mm needles and MC cast on 109(117:125:133) sts.
1st row: K1, p1 to last st, k1.
2nd row: P1, k1 to last st, p1.
These 2 rows form rib. Rep 1st and 2nd rows 14 more times, then 1st row again.
Inc row: rib 9(13:17:21), * inc in next st, rib 5; rep from * ending row rib 9(13:17:21) [(125(133:141:149)) sts].
Change to 3¼mm needles, cont as follows:

1st row: (right side) k.
2nd row: K1, p to last st, k1.
3rd to 12th rows: as 1st and 2nd.

13th row: as 1st.
14th row: K1, p1(5:9:13), B1, * p7, B1; rep from * to last 2(6:10:14 sts), p to last st, k1.
15th and 16th rows: as 1st and 2nd

17th row: as 1st
18th row: k1, p5(9:13:17), B1, * p15, B1; rep from * to last 6(10:14:18) sts, p to last st, k1.
19th and 20th rows: as 1st and 2nd.
21st row: K2 (6:2:6), MB * k7, MB; rep from * to last 2 (6:2:6) sts, k to end.
22nd row: as 2nd.
23rd to 30th rows: as 1st and 2nd.
31st row: K6 (2:6:2), MB, * k7, MB; rep from * to last 6(2:6:2) sts, k to end.
32nd row: as 2nd
33rd and 34th rows: as 1st and 2nd
35th and 36th rows: with C, K.
37th to 42nd rows: as 1st and 2nd
43rd and 44th rows: with C, K.
These 44 rows form pattern.
Rep 1st to 44th rows once, then 1st to 32nd rows again.

Shape Armholes while keeping cont of patt.

Cast off 4 sts at beg of the next 4 rows, then 3 sts at the beg of the foll 4 rows.
Dec 1 st at each end of the next and 1(3:5:7) foll alt rows [93(97:101:105) sts].
Work 43(39:35:31) rows straight.

Shape Neck while keeping cont of patt.

Patt 30(32:34:36), turn, leaving rem sts on a spare needle.
Cont on first sts dec 1 st at the neck edge of the next 15(15:16:16) rows.
Work 6(6:5:5) rows straight.
Cast off.
Rejoin yarn to sts on spare needle.
Patt 33, leave these sts on a st holder, patt to end.
Work rem sts to match the opposite side.

SLEEVES (both alike, all sizes)

With 2¾mm needles and MC cast on 67 sts.
Work 31 rows in rib.
Inc row: rib 8, * inc in next st, rib 2; rep from * ending the row rib 7 (85 sts).
Change to 3¼mm needles.
Cont in patt. foll. 2nd set of figs, work 1st to

44th rows once, then 1st to 32nd rows again (76 rows).

Shape Top while keeping cont of patt.

Cast off 4 sts at the beg of the next 4 rows, then 3 sts at the beg of the foll 4 rows.
Work 2 rows straight.
Dec 1 st at each end of next and every foll 4th row until 33 sts rem. Work 3 rows. Cast off.

NECK EDGE First join one shoulder seam.

With 2¾mm needles and C and RS facing, pick up and k19(20:21:21) sts evenly down one neck edge from open shoulder, k33, pick up and k19(20:21:21) sts to shoulder seam, 19(20:21:21) sts to 2nd st holder, k33, pick up and k20(21:22:22) sts along rem edge.
Work 10 rows in rib. Cast off ribwise.

SHOULDER PADS

With 3¼mm needles and MC cast on 39 sts.
Work a square in rib. Cast off ribwise.

TO MAKE UP

All techniques are listed in 'Tips for the
Professional Finish'.

1) Weave in all ends.
2) Embroider stem of flower with a 'stem
   stitch' and leaves with a 'lazy daisy' stitch.
3) Join remaining shoulder and neck edge.
4) With an invisible seam join sides and
   sleeves.
5) Set in sleeves, with a back stitch gauging
   top to fit armhole.
6) Make 2 ties. Twist tightly together 4 lengths
   of C 360 cm long, let them twist in half to
   finish approx 180 cm.
7) Thread through welt as shown, knot each
   end, tie each into a neat bow.
8) Sew in shoulder pads.

S P R I N G

DESIGN NUMBER 5
'THE CLASSICS' – Sue

Description

Twinset, long cardigan over singlet in Aran patterns.

CARDIGAN AND SINGLET

Materials

Schaffhauser Lambswool 4 ply in 50 gram balls

Cardigan: 11(12:13) balls

Singlet: 8(9:10) balls

1 pair each 2¾mm and 3¼mm needles. A 60cm long circular needle, 2¼mm.

1 cable needle

10 buttons

Measurements

To fit bust

86cm	91cm	96cm

Actual measurements

Cardigan

107cm	112cm	116cm

Singlet

102cm	107cm	112cm

Length to shoulder

Cardigan

66cm	66cm	67cm

Singlet

61cm	61cm	62cm

Length of sleeve

36cm	36cm	36cm

(with turned-back cuff)

Tension

34 sts and 36 rows to 10cm sq measured over pattern on 3¼mm needles.

Special abbreviations for this pattern

C6 = Cable over 6 sts. (Place 3 sts onto cable needle and leave at back of work, k3, then k3 from cable needle.)

C3R = Cross-over to the right using 3 sts. (Place next st onto cable needle and leave at back of work, k2, then p1 from cable needle.)

C3L = Cross-over to the left using 3 sts. (Place next 2 sts onto cable needle and leave at front of work, p1, then k2 from cable needle.)

M3 = Make 3 sts (k1, p1, k1) all into next st.

CARDIGAN

BACK

With 2¾mm needles, cast on 181(189:197) sts.

1st row: K1,* p1, k1; rep from * to end.

2nd row: P1, * k1, p1; rep from * to end.

Rep these 2 rows 6 times more, inc 1 st in centre of last row [182(190:198) sts].

Change to 3¼mm needles and patt.

1st row: K1, p37(41:45), * kb1, p2, k6, p2, kb1, p9, k4, p9, kb1, p2, k6, p2, kb1, * p14; rep from * to *, *** p37(41:45), k1.

2nd row: ** K1, p37(41:45), * pb1, k2, p6, k2, pb1, k9, p4, k9, pb1, k2, p6, k2, pb1, * p14; rep from * to *, *** p37(41:45), k1.

3rd row: K1, p37(41:45), * kb1, p2, C6, p2, kb1, p8, C3R, C3L, p8, kb1, p2, C6, p2, kb1, * p14; rep from * to *, *** p37(41:45), k1.

4th row: ** K1, (M3, p3 tog) 9(10:11) times, k1, * pb1, k2, p6, k2, pb1, k8, p2, k1, p3, k8, pb1, k2, p6, k2, pb1, * k1, (M3, p3 tog) 3 times, k1; rep from * to *, *** k1, (M3, p3 tog) 9(10:11) times, k1.

5th row: K1, p37(41:45), * kb1, p2, k6, p2, kb1, p7, C3R, p1, k1, C3L, p7, kb1, p2, k6, p2, kb1, * p14, rep from * to *, *** p37 (41:45), k1.

6th row: **K1, (p3 tog, M3) 9(10:11) times, k1, * pb1, k2, p6, k2, pb1, k7, p2, (k1, p1) twice, p2, k7, pb1, k2, p6, k2, pb1, * k1, (p3 tog, M3) 3 times, k1; rep from * to *, *** k1, (p3 tog, M3) 9(10:11) times, k1.

7th row: K1, p37(41:45), * kb1, p2, k6, p2, kb1, p6, C3R, (p1, k1) twice, C3L, p6, kb1, p2, k6, p2, kb1, * p14; rep from * to *, *** p37(41:45), k1.

8th row: K1, (M3, p3 tog) 9(10:11) times, k1, * pb1, k2, p6, k2, pb1, k6, p2, (k1, p1) 3 times, p2, k6, pb1, k2, p6, k2, pb1, * k1, (M3, p3 tog) 3 times, k1; rep from * to *, *** k1, (M3, p3 tog) 9(10:11) times, k1.

9th row: K1, p37(41:45), * kb1, p2, k6, p2, kb1, p5, C3R, (p1, k1) 3 times, C3L, p5, kb1, p2, k6, p2, kb1, * p14; rep from * to *, *** p37(41:45), k1.

10th row: ** K1, (p3 tog, M3) 9(10:11) times, k1, * pb1, k2, p6, k2, pb1, k5, p2, (k1, p1) 4 times, p2, k5, pb1, k2, p6, k2, pb1, * k1, (p3 tog, M3) 3 times, k1; rep from * to *, *** k1, (p3 tog, M3) 9(10:11) times, k1.

11th row: K1, p37(41:45), * kb1, p2, C6, p2, C6, p2, kb1, p4, C3R, (p1, k1) 4 times, C3L, p4, kb1, p2, kb1, * p14; rep from * to *, *** p37 (41:45), k1.

12th row: ** k1, (M3, p3 tog) 9(10:11) times, k1, * pb1, k2, p6, k2, pb1, k4, p2, (k1, p1) 5 times, p2, k4, pb1, k2, p6, k2, pb1, * k1, (M3, p3 tog) 3 times, k1; rep from * to *, *** k1, (M3, p3 tog) 9(10:11) times, k1.

13th row: K1, p37(41:45), * kb1, p2, k6, p2, kb1, p3, C3R, (p1, k1) 5 times, C3L, p3, kb1, p2, k6, p2, kb1, * p14; rep from * to *, *** p37(41:45), k1.

14th row: ** k1, (p3 tog, M3) 9(10:11) times, k1, * pb1, k2, p6, k2, pb1, k3, p2, (k1, p1) 6 times, p2, k3, pb1, k2, p6, k2, pb1, * k1, (p3 tog, M3) 3 times, k1; rep from * to *, *** k1, (p3 tog, M3) 9(10:11) times, k1.

15th row: K1, p37(41.45), * kb1, p2, k6, p2, kb1, p3, C3L, (k1, p1) 5 times, C3R, p3, kb1, p2, k6, p2, kb1, * p14; rep from * to *, *** p37(41:45), k1.

16th row: ** k1, (M3, p3 tog) 9(10:11) times, k1, * pb1, k2, p6, k2, pb1, k4, p2, (k1, p1) 5 times, p2, k4, pb1, k2, p6, k2, pb1, * k1, (M3 p3 tog) 3 times, k1; rep from * to *, *** k1, (M3, p3 tog) 9(10:11) times, k1.

17th row: K1, p37(41:45), * kb1, p2, k6, p2, kb1, p4, C3L, (k1, p1) 4 times, C3R, p4, kb1, p2, k6, p2, kb1, * p14; rep from * to *, *** p37(41:45), k1.

18th row: ** k1, (p3 tog, M3) 9(10:11) times, k1, * pb1, k2, p6, k2, pb1, k5, p2, (k1, p1) 4 times, p2, k5, pb1, k2, p6, k2, pb1, * k1, (p3 tog, M3) 3 times, k1; rep from * to *, *** k1, (p3 tog, M3) 9(10:11) times, k1.

19th row: K1, p37(41:45), * kb1, p2, C6, p2,
kb1, p5, C3L, (k1, p1) 3 times, C3R,
p5, kb1, p2, C6, p2, kb1, * p14; rep
from * to *, *** p37(41:45), k1.
20th row: ** k1, (M3, p3 tog) 9(10:11) times,
k1, * pb1, k2, p6, k2, pb1, k6, p2,
(k1, p1) 3 times, p2, k6, pb1, k2, p6,
k2, pb1, * k1, (M3, p3 tog) 3 times,
k1; rep from * to *, *** k1, (M3, p3
tog) 9(10:11) times, k1.
21st row: K1, p37(41:45), * kb1, p2, k6, p2,
kb1, p6, C3L, (k1, p1) twice, C3R,
p6, kb1, p2, k6, p2, kb1, p14; rep
from * to *, *** p37(41:45), k1.
22nd row: ** k1, (p3 tog, M3) 9(10:11) times,
k1, * pb1, k2, p6, k2, pb1, k7, p2,
(k1, p1) twice, p2, k7, pb1, k2, p6,
k2, pb1, * k1, (p3 tog, M3) 3 times,
k1; rep from * to *, *** k1, (p3 tog,
M3) 9(10:11) times, k1.
23rd row: K1, p37(41:45), * kb1, p2, k6, p2,
kb1, p7, C3L, k1, p1, C3R, p7, kb1,
p2, k6, p2, kb1, * p14; rep from * to
*, *** p37 (41:45), k1.
24th row: ** k1, (M3, p3 tog) 9(10:11) times,
k1, * pb1, k2, p6, k2, pb1, k8, p2,
k1, p3, k8, pb1, k2, p6, k2, pb1, *
k1, (M3, p3 tog) 3 times, k1; rep
from * to *, *** k1, (M3, p3 tog)
9(10:11) times, k1.
25th row: K1, p37(41:45), * kb1, p2, k6, p2,
kb1, p8, C3L, C3R, p8, kb1, p2, k6,
p2, kb1, * p14; rep from * to *, ***
p37(41:45), k1.
26th row: ** k1, (p3 tog, M3) 9(10:11) times,
k1, * pb1, k2, p6, k2, pb1, k9, p4,
k9, pb1, k2, p6, k2, pb1, * k1, (p3
tog, M3) 3 times, k1; rep from * to
*, *** k1, (p3 tog, M3) 9(10:11)
times, k1.

The 3rd to 26th rows form the pattern.
Rep the 3rd to 26th rows 4 times more, then
the 3rd to 20th rows again.

Shape armholes

While keeping patt correct, cast off 5 sts at beg
of next 2 rows, then 4 sts at beg of foll 4 rows.
Dec 1 st at each end of the next 14(16:18) rows,
then 1 st each end of the foll 5(7:5) RS rows
[118(118:126) sts]. Cont straight until Back
measures 23(23:24)cm from beg of armhole
shaping, ending with a WS row.

Shape shoulders

Cast off 10 sts at the beg of the next 4 rows,
then 9(9:11) sts at beg of foll 2 rows. Leave the
rem 60(60:64) sts on a holder for back neck.

RIGHT FRONT

With 2¾mm needles, cast on 99(103:107) sts and work 8 rows in rib as given for Back.

1st buttonhole row: RS Rib 4, cast off the next 4 sts, rib to end.

2nd buttonhole row: Rib to last 4 sts, cast on 4, rib to end.

Work 3 more rows in rib.
Next row: Rib to last 12 sts and turn, leaving the 12sts on a holder [87(91:95) sts].
Change to 3¼mm needles and cont in patt as follows.

1st row: K1, p2, work as for 1st row on Back from * to *, p37(41:45), k1.
2nd row: Work as for 2nd row on Back from ** to second *, k3.
3rd row: K1, p2, work as for 3rd row on Back from * to *, p37(41:45), k1.
4th row: Work as for 4th row on Back from ** to second *, k3.

These 4 rows establish the patt for Right Front **** Cont in this way until 26 rows of patt have been completed.

Rep the 3rd to 26th rows 4 times more, then the 3rd to 21st (work 20 rows here for Left Front) rows again.

Shape armhole

Cast off 5 sts at the beg of the next row, then 4 sts at beg of foll 2 alt rows.

Dec 1 st at this same edge on the next 14(16:18) rows, then 1 st on the foll 5(7:5) RS rows [55(55:59) sts].
Cont straight until Front measures 10cm from beg of armhole shaping, ending with a WS row. Mark end of last row with a contrast thread (mark beg of last row for Left Front), to indicate beg of neck shaping.
Dec 1 st at the neck edge on the next and every foll RS row until 29(29:31) sts rem. Work straight until Front measures the same as Back to back neck sts, ending at the armhole edge. Cast off.

LEFT FRONT

With 2¾mm needles, cast on 99(103:107) sts and work 13 rows in rib as given for Back.
Next row: Rib 12sts and place them onto a holder, rib to end. Change to 3¼mm needles and cont in patt as follows.
1st row: Work as for 1st row on Back to second *, p2, k1.
2nd row: K3, work as for 2nd row on Back from * to *, p37(41:45), k1.

3rd row: Work as for 3rd row on Back to second *, p2, k1.
4th row: K3, work as for 4th row on Back from * to *, p37(41:45), k1.

These 4 rows establish the patt for Left Front. Complete as for Right Front from **** noting the bracketed exceptions.

SLEEVES (both alike)

With 2¾mm needles, cast on 85(85:93) sts and work 28 rows in rib as given for back.
Inc row: Rib 2(2:6), * inc into next st, rib 3; rep from * to last 3(3:7) sts, inc into next st, rib 2(2:6) [106(106:114)sts].
Change to 3¼mm needles and set the patt as follows.

1st row: K1, p29(29:33), work as for 1st row on Back from * to *, p29(29:33), k1.
2nd row: K1, p29(29:33), work as for 2nd row on Back from * to *, p29(29:33), k1.
3rd row: K1, p29(29:33), work as for 3rd row on Back from * to *, p29(29:33), k1.
4th row: K1, (M3, p3 tog) 7(7:8) times, k1, work as for 4th row on Back from * to *, k1, (M3, p3 tog) 7(7:8) times, k1.
5th row: K1, p29(29:33), work as for 5th row on Back from * to *, p29(29:33), k1.
6th row: K1, (p3 tog, M3) 7(7:8) times, k1, work as for 6th row on Back from * to *, k1, (p3 tog, M3) 7(7:8) times, k1.

These 6 rows establish the sleeve patt.
Cont to work in patt as set, inc and working into side patt, one st at each end of the next and every foll 3rd row until 170(170:178) sts are on the needle.

Work 16 rows straight, thus ending with the 20th row patt.

Shape sleeve top

Whilst keeping patt correct, cast off 5 sts at beg of next 2 rows, then 4 sts at beg of foll 4 rows.
Next row: Work to end, dec 1 st at each end of row.
Next row: Work to end.
Next row: Work to end, dec 1 st at each end of row.

Rep the last 3 rows until 76 sts rem, thus ending with a WS row.
Cast off 4 sts at beg of next 6 rows. Cast off the rem 52 sts knitting 2 tog across the row (26 cast-off sts).

BUTTONHOLE BAND

Return to the 12 sts on holder for Right Front. With WS facing and using 2¾mm needles, join in yarn at inside edge and Work 13 rows in rib.
Next 2 rows: Work the 2 buttonhole rows as given for Right Front.
Work 16 rows in rib.
Rep the last 18 rows 7 times more, then work 2 more buttonhole rows.
Cont in rib only until band is long enough to reach up Front and round to centre back neck, when slightly stretched. Cast off ribwise.

BUTTON BAND

Return to the 12 sts on holder for Left Front. With RS facing, join in yarn at inside edge and work in rib until band is long enough to reach centre back neck. Cast off ribwise.

SHOULDER PADS

With 3¼mm needles, cast on 41 sts and work a square in rib. Cast off ribwise.

TO MAKE UP

All required techniques are listed in 'Tips for the Professional Finish'.

1) Weave in ends.
2) Join shoulders.
3) With an invisible seam, join centre back seam of front bands.
4) With an invisible seam, sew band in place.
5) With an invisible seam, join sides and sleeves.

6) Set in sleeves, gauging top to fit armholes.
7) Sew shoulder pads in place.
8) Sew buttons to left front band to correspond with buttonholes.

SINGLET

BACK

With 2¾mm needles, cast on 141(149:157) sts and work 21 rows in rib as given for Cardigan Back.
Inc row: Rib 6(10:14), * inc into next st, rib 3; rep from * to last 3(7:11) sts, rib to end [174(182:190) sts].
Change to 3¼mm needles and set the patt as follows.
1st row: K1, p33(37:41), work as for 1st row on Cardigan Back from * to ***, p33(37:41), k1.
2nd row: K1, p33(37:41), work as for 2nd row on Cardigan Back from * to ***, p33(37:41), k1.
3rd row: K1, p33(37:41), work as for 3rd row on Cardigan Back from * to ***, p33(37:41), k1.
4th row: K1, (M3, p3 tog) 8(9:10) times, k1, work as for 4th row on Cardigan Back from * to ***, k1, (M3, p3 tog) 8(9:10) times, k1.
5th row: K1, p33(37:41), work as for 5th row on Cardigan Back from * to ***, p33(37:41), k1.
6th row: K1, (p3 tog, M3) 8(9:10) times, k1, work as for 6th row on Cardigan Back from * to ***, k1, (p3 tog, M3) 8(9:10) times, k1.

These 6 rows establish the patt for Singlet Back. Cont in this way until 26 rows of patt have been worked.
Rep the 3rd to 26th rows 3 times more, then the 3rd to 20th rows again.

Shape armholes

Whilst keeping patt correct, cast off 5 sts at beg of next 2 rows, then 4 sts at beg of foll 4 rows.
Dec 1 st at each end of the next 12(16:20) rows, then 1 st each end of the foll 15(14:13) RS rows [94(96:98) sts]. ****
Work straight until Back measures 19(19:21) cm from beg of armhole shaping, ending with a WS row.

Shape back neck

Next row: While keeping patt correct, work 19(20:21) sts and turn, leaving the rem sts on a spare needle. Cont on this first set of sts.
Dec1 st at the neck edge on the next 7 rows.

Cont straight until work measures 23(23:24) cm from beg of armhole shaping, end with a WS row.
Cast off the rem 12(13:14) sts.
With RS facing, join in yarn to rem sts at neck edge, cast off 56 sts and patt to end.
Complete to match opposite side of neck.

FRONT

Work as for Back to ****
Cont straight until Front measures 15(15:16) cm from beg of armhole shaping, ending with a WS row.
Shape neck and complete as for Back.

NECK EDGING

Join both shoulder seams.
With RS facing and using the 2¾mm circular needle and commencing at right shoulder seam pick up and k156 sts evenly around neck edge.
Work 10 rounds in k1 p1 rib. Cast off loosely ribwise.

ARMHOLE EDGINGS (both alike)

With RS facing and using 2¾mm needles, pick up and k129(129:135) sts evenly around armhole edge.
Work 10 rows in rib, dec 1 st at each end of every RS row. Cast off loosely ribwise.

TO MAKE UP

All required techniques are listed in 'Tips for the Professional Finish'.

1) Weave in ends.
2) With an invisible seam, sew side seams and short edges of armbands.

SPRING

Description

Loose-fitting long-sleeve sweater worked in stocking stitch and reverse stocking stitch panels with collar and seam details.

Materials

Twilleys Pegasus 8 ply Cotton 11(12) × 50 gram balls.

One pair each needles sizes 4mm and 3¼mm and 4mm circular needle

Measurements

To fit chest
92–96cm   102–107cm

Actual measurements
117cm   122cm

Length from shoulder
67cm   70cm

Sleeve seam
51cm   53cm

Tension

18 sts and 24 rows to 10cm sq measured over st st on 4mm needles.

Stitches Used

St st

Row 1: Knit.
Row 2: Purl.
Repeat these 2 rows.

Rev st st

Row 1: Purl.
Row 2: Knit.
Repeat these 2 rows.

K1 p1 rib

Row 1: * k1 p1 *
Row 2: P the k sts and k the p sts of previous row.
Repeat these two rows.

BACK piece 1

With 3¼mm needles cast on 95(99) sts and work in k1 p1 rib for 9cm.
Inc row: Rib 7(5), *inc into next st, rib 8(7), rep from * 9(11) times, inc into next st, rib to end [105(111) sts].
Change to 4mm needles and work in st st (first row knit) until work measures 28(29)cm from cast-on edge. Cast off evenly.

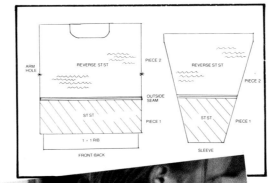

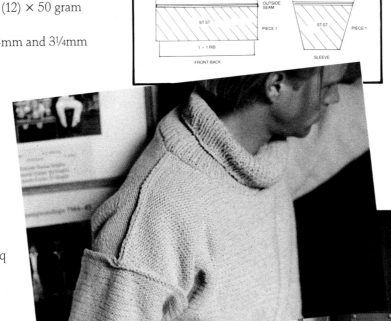

KNITTING STANDARD

BACK piece 2

With 4mm needles cast on 105(111) sts and work in rev st st (first row purl) until work measures 13(13)cm.
Mark each end of next row with a coloured thread to indicate armhole position. ***
Continue until work measures 39(41)cm from cast-on edge. Cast off.

FRONT piece 1

Work as for piece 1 of back

FRONT piece 2

Work as for piece 2 of back to ***
Continue until work measures 31(32)cm from cast-on edge.

With right side of work facing divide for neck shaping as follows:
Purl 45(47), cast off centre 15(17) sts, purl 45(47).
Work on each set of sts in turn as follows:
* Cast off 2 sts at neck edge, then dec 1 st at neck edge on foll row *
Repeat from * to * once more [39(41) sts].
Cast off 2 sts at neck edge on next 2 alt rows, then dec 1 st at neck edge on the foll 3 alt rows.
Work without further shaping on 32(34) sts until work measures 39(41)cm, from cast-on edge. Cast off.
Work other side to match reversing all shapings.

SLEEVES (2 alike with 2 pieces each sleeve)

Piece 1

With 4mm needles cast on 44(48) sts and work in st st for 5 cm.
Now inc 1 st at each end of next and every foll 4th row until 68(72) sts are reached.
Continue straight until work measures 24(26)cm. Cast off.

Piece 2

With 4mm needles cast on 68(72) sts and work in rev st st for 2 rows.
Now inc 1 st at each end of next and every foll 4th row until 94(98) sts are reached. Continue straight until work measures 27(28)cm from cast-on edge. Cast off.
Work 2 more pieces for other sleeve.

COLLAR

Using 4mm circular needle cast on 108(116) sts and work in k1 p1 rib for 18cm.
Cast off ribwise.

TO MAKE UP

Refer to 'Tips for the Professional Finish'.

1) Weave in all ends (taking care to work on WS of each piece).
2) Block and pin.
3) Press, omitting all ribbing.
4) Join bottom and top pieces of back, front and sleeves by back stitch with the seam on the outside, taking care to keep straight.
5) Join shoulder seams on the inside.
6) Place top of sleeves between the coloured markers and sew on the inside.
7) Join side seams and sleeve seam on the inside.
8) Fix circular collar and join to neck with an inside seam.
9) Turn back cuffs.

SPRING

Description

Fair Isle sweater with zip neck and yoke, striped body over ribbed leggings.

Materials

Lister Lee Montoravia DK

SWEATER MC – (lemon) 8(9:10:11) × 50 gram balls
C – (lilac) 6(7:8:9) × 50 gram balls
BODY WARMER MC – 1(1:1:1) × 50 gram ball.
C – 1(1:1:1) × 50 gram ball
LEGGINGS 8(9:10:11) × 50 gram balls

One pair each needles sizes 3¼mm and 4mm, 1 circular needle size 3¼mm for leggings.

1 20cm zip for collar, 1 30cm open-ended zip for bodywarmer. Elastic 5cm wide to fit waist, for the leggings.

Measurements

To fit bust

81cm	86cm	91cm	96cm

Actual measurements

97cm	101cm	106cm	112cm

Length from shoulder

43cm	43cm	44cm	44cm

Sleeve seam (approx)

31cm	31cm	31cm	31cm

Leggings to fit hips

86cm	91cm	96cm	101cm

Tension

24sts and 28 rows to 10 cm measured over patt in st st on size 4mm needles.

BACK

With 3¼mm needles and MC cast on 117(123:129:135) sts.
1st row: K1, p1 to last st, k1.
2nd row: P1, k1 to last st, p1.
These 2 rows form rib. Rep these 2 rows 9 more times (20 rows).
Change to 4mm needles.
Cont in st st foll patt set on chart for 40 rows.

Shape Armhole while keeping cont of patt.

Cast off 4 sts at the beg of the next 4 rows.
Dec 1 st at each end of the next 2(3:5:7) rows,

work 0(1:1:1) rows.
Dec on next and 2 foll alt rows [91(95:97:99) sts] **.
Work straight until back measures 22(22:23:23)cm from beg of armhole shaping, ending with a wrong side row.

Shape Shoulders while keeping cont of patt.

Cast off 11 sts at the beg of the next 2 rows, then 9(10:10:10) sts at the beg of foll 2 rows [51(53:55:57) sts].
Leave these sts on a st holder.

FRONT

Work as back to **
Work 5 rows straight.

Shape Neck while keeping cont of patt.
Patt 45(47:48:49),turn, leaving rem on a spare needle.
Cont on first sts.
Dec 1 st at the neck edge of the foll 2 rows, work 1 row straight.
Cont in this way, dec 1 st at the neck edge on 2 out of every 3 rows until 20(21:21:21) sts rem.
Work straight until front matches back at longest point. Cast off.
Rejoin yarn to sts on spare needle.
Cast off centre stitch, patt to end.
Work rem sts to match opposite side.

SLEEVES (both alike)

With 3¼mm needles and MC cast on 65(65:69:69) sts.
Cont working in rib as follows:
1st to 4th rows: with MC
5th and 6th rows: with C
Work 19 rows in rib as set.
Inc row: with MC rib 1(1:3:3) * inc in next st, rib 2; rep from * ending the row inc in next st, rib 0(0:2:2) [87(87:91:91) sts].
Change to 4mm needles.
Cont in st st foll patt set on chart, inc 1 st at each end of every 3rd row while keeping cont of patt, until there are 119(119:123:123) sts on the needle.
Work 22 rows straight.

Shape Top while keeping cont of patt.
Cast off 4 sts at the beg of the next 4 rows.
Dec 1 st at each end of the next and every foll alt row until 61 sts rem. Cast off 3 sts at the beg of the foll 4 rows.
Cast off the rem. sts.

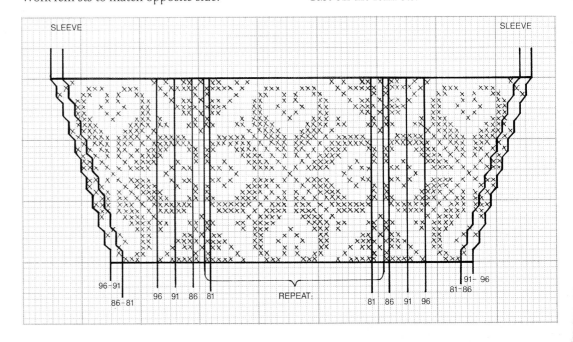

NECK EDGE

First join both shoulder seams.
With a 3¼mm circular needle and MC pick up and k45(45:47:47) sts from right side of cast-off sts, along right neck edge to shoulder seam, k51(53:55:57), pick up and k45(45:47:47) sts down left neck edge.
Working to and fro across needle, not in rounds, work 20 rows in striped rib as set for cuffs, dec 1 st at each end of every row.

COLLAR

Cont straight on rem sts, keeping cont of striped rib for 24 rows, K wrong side row to mark edge.
Work 24 more rows in striped rib. Cast off ribwise.

SHOULDER PADS (make 2)

With 3¼mm needles and MC cast on 39 sts.
Work a square in rib. Cast off ribwise.

TO MAKE UP All techniques are in 'Tips for the Professional Finish'

1) Weave in all ends.
2) Omitting ribs, block out and press.
3) With an invisible seam join sides and sleeves.
4) Sew zip in place, turn collar along edge to WS, slip stitch in place.
5) With a back stitch set in sleeves, gauging top to fit armhole.
6) Sew in shoulder pads.

BODYWARMER

With 4mm needles and MC cast on 179(189:201:211) sts.
Work 54 rows in striped rib.
Change to 3¼mm needles cont in striped rib for 34 rows.
Cast off ribwise.

TO COMPLETE

1) Weave in ends.
2) Sew in open-ended zip.

LEGGINGS

Right Leg

With 3¼mm needles cast on 67(71:79:87) sts.
1st row: K1, p1 to last st, k1.
2nd row: P1, k1 to last st, p1.
These 2 rows form the rib. Rep 1st and 2nd rows 8 more times (18 rows).
Change to 4mm needles.
Cont in rib inc 1 st at each end of every foll 6th row until there are 111(117:127:135) sts on the needle.
Work 1 row.

Now inc on next and every foll alt row until there are 131(137:149:159) sts.
Work 2 rows straight.

Shape Crotch while keeping the cont of rib.
Cast off 5 sts at the beg of the next row, 7 sts at the beg of the foll row and 3 sts at the beg of the foll 4 rows.
Dec 1 st at each end of the next and foll alt row.
Work 1 row.
Next row rib dec last st.
Rep the last 2 rows 3(3:5:5) times [99(105:115:125) sts].
Work 15(19:21:23) rows straight.
Next row: rib 47(50:55:60), dec 1, rib 1, dec 1, rib 47(50:55:60).
Work 3 rows straight.
Foll row: rib 46(49:54:59), dec 1, rib 1, dec 1, rib 46(49:54:59).

Work 3 rows straight.
Cont in this way dec 1 st either side of centre st on next and every 4th row until 79(85:93:101) sts rem.
Work 4 rows straight.

Shape Waist while keeping cont of rib.
1st row: rib 70, turn, rib right side row
3rd row: rib 58, turn, rib right side row
5th row: rib 46, turn, rib right side row
7th row: rib 34, turn, rib right side row
9th row: rib 24, turn, rib right side row
11th row: rib 14, turn, rib right side row
13th row: rib 7, turn, rib right side row
15th row: rib 7, turn, rib right side row
Leave the sts on a spare needle.

Left Leg
Beg with 2nd row of rib work as right reversing the shapings.

TO COMPLETE

All the techniques are given in 'Tips for the Professional Finish'.

1) Sew in all ends
2) With an invisible seam join inner legs
3) With a back stitch join the shaped part of the crotch. This will reinforce the seam.
4) With an invisible seam join rem part of crotch.

WAIST BAND

With a 3¼mm circular needle work in rounds for 6 cm in rib.
Cast off loosely ribwise.
Weave in ends.
Make a herringbone casing over the elastic.

SPRING

Description

Saddle-shoulder sweater worked in stocking stitch with 'shaped hem' and deep rounded neck details, with calf-length skirt with shaped hip and waist details.

Materials

Tootal Nougat – pistachio

Top: 8(9) × 50 gram balls

Skirt: 7(8) × 50 gram balls

One pair each needles sizes 5mm and 4mm, 3¾mm and 3¼mm and a stitch holder.

Elastic (6cm wide) to fit waist.

Top Measurements

To fit bust
86–91cm   91–97cm

Actual measurements
91cm   97cm

Length at back
43cm   46cm

Sleeve seam (approx)
45cm   47cm

Skirt Measurements

To fit hip
86–91cm   91–97cm

Finished measurement
86cm   91cm

Length
79cm   84cm

Tension

19 sts and 26 rows to 10cm sq measured over st st on 5mm

TOP

BACK

With 5mm needles cast on 12(14) sts and work in st st.
Work 2 rows then form shaped back by casting on 6(6) sts at beg of next 6 rows, then 7(8) sts at beg of next 6 rows, then 4(4) at beg of next 2 rows [90(94) sts].
Mark each end of last row with a coloured thread.
Work in st st without further shaping until work measures 13(14)cm from coloured marker.

Shape Armhole

Cast off 3 sts at beg of next 2 rows, then dec 1 st at each end of the next 2 rows, then dec 1 st at each end of the next 2 foll alt rows [76(80) sts].
Continue without further shaping until work measures 29(30)cm from coloured marker.
Cast off.

THE FRONT

Left side

With 5mm needles cast on 45(47) sts and working in st st shape front as follows (mark first st with a coloured thread):

Row 1:   K4, turn, sl1, purl to end.
Row 3:   K11(12) (taking a further 7(8) sts into work), turn, sl1, purl to end.
Row 5:   K18(20), turn, sl1, purl to end.
Row 7:   K24(26), turn, sl1, purl to end.
Row 9:   K28(30), turn, sl1, purl to end.
Row 11: K45(47), turn, sl1, purl to end.
Leave these stitches on a spare needle.

Right side

Work another piece as for left, reversing all shapings, ending right side facing.
Now work across all 90(94) sts until work measures 13(14)cm from coloured thread on side seam.

Shape Armholes

Cast off 3 sts at each end of next 2 rows, then dec 1 st at each end of next 2 rows, then dec 1 st at each end of next 2 foll alt rows [76(80) sts].

Shape Neck

Next row: K32(33), cast off centre 12(14) sts, k32(33).
Now work on each side of neck in turn.
Keeping armhole edge straight shape neck by dec 1 st on next row, then cast off 2 sts at neck edge on next 3 alt rows, then dec 1 st on foll 4th rows twice [15(16) sts].
Work should now measure 29(30)cm from marker.
Cast off.
Rejoin yarn and work other side to match, reversing all shapings.

SLEEVES

Left

With 3¾mm needles cast on 50(54) sts and work in k2 p2 rib for 20 rows.
Change to 4mm needles and continue in k2 p2 rib, increasing 1 st at each end of next and every foll 6th row until 62(66) sts are reached.
Change to 5mm and working in st st inc 1 st at each end of every foll 4th row until 86(90) sts are reached.
Continue without further shaping until work measures 45(47)cm from cast-on edge.

Shape sleeve head and yoke

Cast off 3 sts at beg of next 2 rows, then dec 1 st at each end of every row until 66(70) sts remain.
Now dec 1 st at each end of every alt row until 48(52) sts remain.
With right side facing cast off 2 sts at beg of next 6 rows [36(40) sts].
Continue straight for a further 8cm, ending wrong side facing ***
Cast off 18(20) sts, purl to end.
Continue in st st for a further 13(14)cm.
Cast off.

Right sleeve

Work as for left to ***
Reverse top shaping as follows:
With **right side** facing cast off 18(20) sts, knit to end.
Complete to match left sleeve.

TO MAKE UP

Refer to 'Tips for the Professional Finish'.

1) Weave in all ends.
2) Block and pin and steam.
3) With an invisible seam sew the cast-off edges of each sleeve tog to form 'centre back' of back yoke.
4) Sew back yoke to back and each sleeve head to back with invisible seams.
5) With an invisible seam sew front to '8cm section' of sleeve head to form front yoke, and sleeve heads to front at either side.

KNITTING STANDARD ✕

COLLAR

Starting at 'centre back' of neck pick up 156(160) sts evenly along the 13(14)cm section, down side of neck, across cast-off sts at front, and round other side to back of neck.
Using 4mm needles work in k2 p2 rib for 4cm, then change to 3¾mm needles and rib as set for a further 4cm, then change to 3¼mm needles and rib for a further 1cm.
Cast off firmly in rib.

BOTTOM RIB

With an invisible seam sew one side seam. Beginning at other side edge pick up 172(176) sts and using 4mm needles work in k2 p2 rib for 6cm, then change to 3¾mm needles and rib for a further 1cm.
Cast off firmly in rib.

TO FINISH

1) Sew side seam with an invisible seam.
2) With invisible seams sew sleeve seams.

SKIRT

Using 4mm needles cast on 76(78) sts and work k2 p2 rib for 8 rows.
Change to 5mm needles and work in st st, increasing 1 st at each end of the foll 42nd rows 3 times.
Continue on these 82(84) sts until work measures 61(63)cm.

Shaping to waist

Dec 1 st at each end of next and foll 6th row until 76(80) sts are reached, then dec 1 st at each end of every foll 4th row until 68(70) sts remain, leave sts on a stitch holder.
Work another piece the same.

Referring to 'Tips for the Professional Finish'

Sew tog one side seam with an invisible seam. With 4mm needles work across all 136(140) sts in k2 p2 rib for 15cm.
Cast off in rib.

TO MAKE UP

Refer to 'Tips for the Professional Finish'.

1) Weave in all ends.
2) Block and pin and steam.
3) With an invisible seam sew tog other side seam.
4) Turn work to inside and put in elastic referring to method 2, folding waistband to form a hem and slip stitch into place.

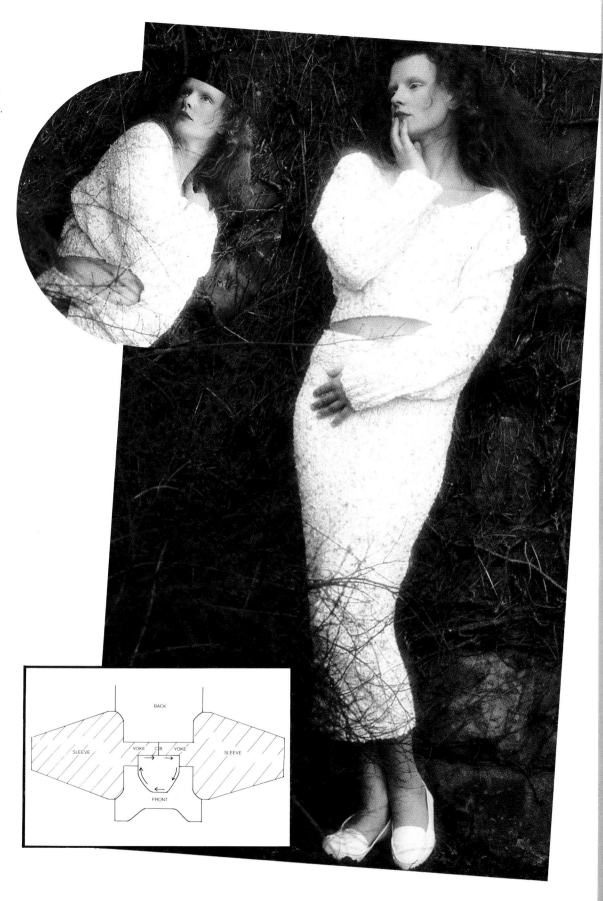

"Those Latins all dream in the sun and indulge their senses"
Tennessee Williams

SUMMER

Button front sweater with side vent details

...kn top to wear as vest or dress

cardigan can be worn with buttons
at front or back

THE PATTERNS

KNITTING STANDARD

Description

Drop shoulder, low 'V' neck cardigan worked in 7 × 7 rib with breast pocket and saddle shoulder details.

Materials

Patons Cotton Perlé Ecru 17(18) × 50 gram balls

One pair each needles sizes 4mm and 3¼mm and spare needles.

3 Buttons

Measurements

To fit chest
91–97cm   102–107cm

Actual measurements
119cm   127cm

Length from shoulder
69cm   71cm

Sleeve seam
48cm   51cm

Tension

24 sts and 29 rows to 10cm sq measured over 7 × 7 rib on 4mm needles.

Stitches Used

1 × 1 Rib

1st Row: * k1, p1 *
2nd Row: K the p sts and p the k sts of previous row.
Repeat these 2 rows.

7 × 7 Rib

1st Row: * k7, p7 *
2nd Row: K the p sts and p the k sts of previous row.
Repeat these 2 rows.

BACK

With 3¼mm needles cast on 141(153) sts and work in k1 p1 rib for 8cm.
Change to 4mm and work in 7 × 7 rib, setting pattern as follows:

1st size: K4, * p7, k7, rep from * to last 11 sts, p7, k4.

2nd size: P3, * k7, p7, rep from * to last 10 sts, k7, p3.
Work in rib as now set until work measures 38(41)cm from cast-on edge.
Place coloured threads at each end of next row to indicate armhole positions.
Continue in rib patt until work measures 60(62)cm. Cast off.

POCKET LININGS (2 alike)

Using 4mm needles cast on 35 sts and work in 7 × 7 rib for 16cm, leaving sts on a spare needle.

RIGHT FRONT

Using 3¼mm needles cast on 60(68) sts and work in k1 p1 rib for 8cm.
Change to 4mm and set 7 × 7 rib as follows:

1st size: * k7, p7, rep from * to last 4 sts, k4.
2nd size: * k7, p7, rep from * to last 12 sts, k7, p5
Continue straight in rib pattern until work measures 26(28)cm from cast-on edge.
Shape neck by dec 1 st at neck edge on next and foll alt row, then dec 1 st at neck edge on the foll 4th rows 8 times, on the foll 6th rows 3 times and foll 8th rows 4 times.

At the same time when work measures 36(38)cm from cast-on edge work pocket top as follows:
With right side facing pattern 13, work next 35 sts in k1 p1 rib, patt 11(12).
Continue working the 35 sts in k1 p1 rib to form pocket top for 3cm.
Next row: Patt, casting off 35 sts of pocket top in knit.
Continue in rib patt as set working sts from pocket lining in place of those cast off in previous row, taking care to match ribs correctly.
When work measures 38(41)cm from cast-on edge place a coloured thread at side to indicate armhole position.
Continue in 7 × 7 rib working neck shaping as stated. When all decreases are worked continue straight until work measures 60(62)cm. Cast off.

LEFT FRONT

Work as for right front reversing all shapings and placing 7 × 7 rib pattern as follows:-
With right side facing:

1st size: K4, * p7, k7, rep from * to end.
2nd size: P5, * k7, p7, rep from * to last 7 sts, k7.

RIGHT SLEEVE

With 3¼mm needles cast on 68(74) sts and work in k1 p1 rib for 8cm.
Change to 4mm needles and set 7 × 7 rib as follows:-

1st size: P6, * k7, p7, rep from * to last 6 sts, k6.
2nd size: K2, * p7, k7, rep from * to last 2 sts, p2.
Continue in 7 × 7 rib as set increasing 1 st at each end of every 3rd row until 130(140) sts are reached, working extra stitches into pattern.
Continue without further shaping until work measures 48(51) cm.

Shape sleeve head

With right side facing cast off 44(49) sts at beg of next 2 rows.

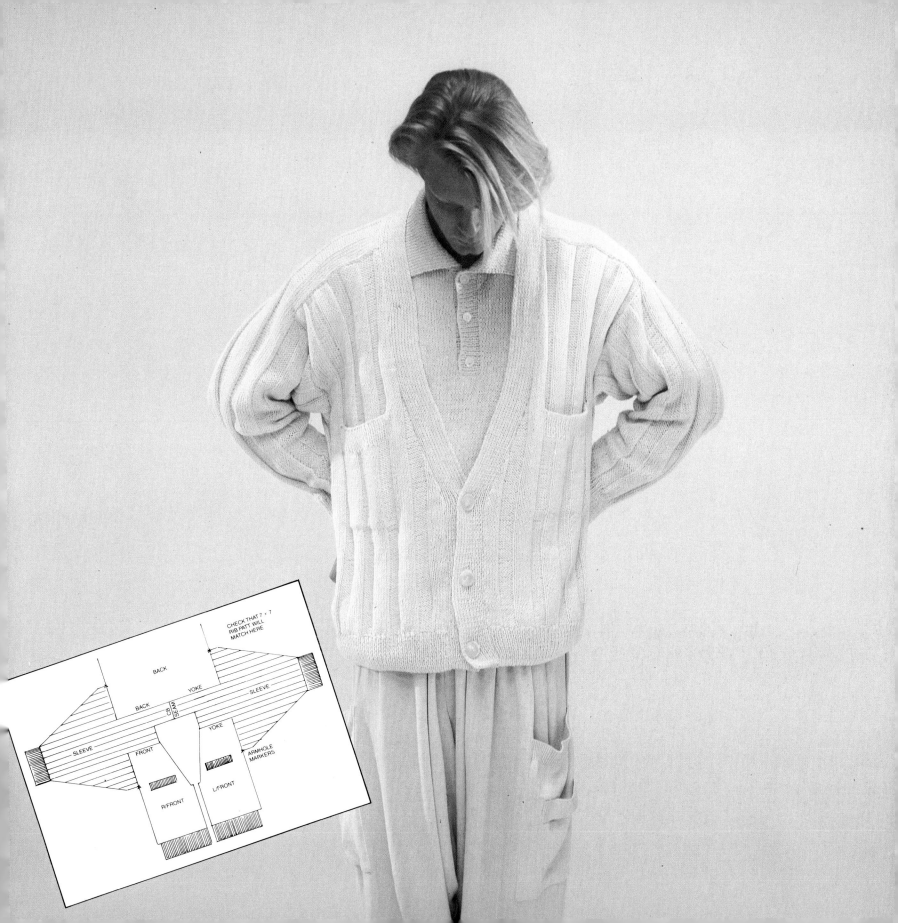

CHECK THAT 7 × 7
RIB PATT WILL
MATCH HERE

BACK

BACK   YOKE   SLEEVE

C.B. SEAM

YOKE

SLEEVE   FRONT

ARMHOLE
MARKERS

R/FRONT   L/FRONT

Work on remaining 42 sts for a further 20(21)cm ending with right side facing ***
Cast off 21 sts at beg of next row and work on remaining 21 sts for a further 9(10)cm. Cast off.

LEFT SLEEVE

Work as for right sleeve but place rib patt as follows:

1st size: K6, * p7, k7, rep from * to last 6 sts, p6.

2nd size: P2, * k7, p7, rep from * to last 2 sts, k2.

Continue as for right sleeve reversing the shaping at sleeve head from ***
i.e. With wrong side facing cast off 21 sts, etc. Make sure ribs match when 21 st portions meet at centre back of neck (this forms back yoke).

TO MAKE UP

Refer to 'Tips for the Professional Finish'.

1) Weave in all ends (taking care to work on wrong side of fabric).
2) Block and pin.
3) Press 7× 7 rib patt gently, allowing patt to 'flatten' slightly, and omitting 1× 1 rib welts.
4) With invisible seam sew cast-off edges of '21 st section' of sleeves tog to form back yoke.
5) With an invisible seam sew back yoke to back.
6) Sew pocket linings to inside of fronts with slip stitch.
7) Sew front yokes to front sections with invisible stitch.
8) Open work out flat and set in sleeves with an invisible seam between armhole markers.
9) Using back stitch sew sleeve seams, with invisible stitch sew side seams.

BUTTONHOLE BAND

Using 3¼mm needles cast on 14 sts and work in k1 p1 rib.
When work measures 4cm make 1st buttonhole as follows:
With right side facing rib 5, cast off next 4 sts, rib 5
Next row: Rib 5, cast on 4 sts over those cast off in previous row, rib 5
Cont in rib, working a further 2 buttonholes at intervals of 9(10)cm.
Now cont in rib until band is long enough, when slightly stretched, to go up length of left front ending at centre back (tack as you work to ensure a good fit!).

BUTTONBAND

Work another piece alike to go up right front, but omit buttonholes.

TO FINISH

With invisible stitch or slip stitch sew bands into position and with invisible stitch join tog bands at centre back. Sew on buttons.

'MODA SHIRT'

KNITTING STANDARD

Description

Loose, easy-fitting, sport-style sweater worked in stocking stitch and 1 × 1 rib in cotton, with button placket, breast pocket and collar details.

Materials

Patons Cotton Perlé 12(12:13) × 50 gram balls

One pair each needles sizes 4mm and 3¼mm and 2¾mm

3 buttons

Measurements

To fit chest

91–97cm	97cm–101cm	101cm–107cm

Actual measurements

112cm	117cm	122cm

Length from shoulder

66cm	69cm	71cm

Sleeve seam

25cm	27cm	28cm

Tension

22 sts and 29 rows to 10cm sq over st st on 4mm needles.

BACK

*** Using 3¼mm needles cast on 121(127:133) sts.

Row 1: K2, * p1, k1, rep from * to last st, k1.
Row 2: * k1, p1, rep from * to last st, k1.
Repeat these 2 rows for 2.5cm, ending with a 2nd row.
Change to 4mm needles and stocking stitch and work until the back measures (39:41:43)cm from cast-on edge, ending with a purl row ***
Mark each end of next row with a coloured thread to indicate armhole position.
Continue in st st until work measures (64:66:69)cm, ending with a purl row.

Shape shoulders

Cast off at beg of next and foll alt rows [14(15:15)] sts 4(4:2) times, then 15(15:16) sts at beg of next foll alt rows 2(2:4) times.
Work 1 row and cast off remaining 35(37:39) sts.

Pocket lining (all sizes)

With 4mm needles cast on 27 sts and work in st st for 13cm, ending on a purl row, leaving sts on a spare needle.

FRONT

Work as for back from *** to ***, ending with a knit row.
Mark each end of next row with a coloured thread to indicate armholes.

Next row: P77(81:85) sts, cast off next 27 sts, purl to end.
Next row: K17(19:21) sts, k27 sts of pocket lining in place of those cast off in previous row, k to end.

Work in st st until work measures 43(44:46)cm, ending with a purl row.

Next row: K56(59:62), cast off next 9 sts, knit to end.

Turn and work on this set of sts until work measures 59(61:64)cm, ending with a purl row.

Shape neck

Cast off 4(5:6) sts at beg of next row and shape as follows:
Dec 1 st at neck edge on next 6 rows, then dec 1 st at neck edge on next foll alt 4 rows [43(45:47) sts].
Work 2 rows.
With right side of work facing shape shoulder by casting off 14(15:15) sts at beg of the next and foll alt row 2(2:1) times, then 15(15:16) sts at beg of foll alt row 1(1:2) times.
Rejoin yarn to other set of sts and work left front to match right front reversing all shapings.

SLEEVES (2 alike)

Using 3¼mm needles cast on 78(82:88) sts.

Row 1: K2, * p1, k1, rep from * to last st, k1.
Row 2: * k1, p1, rep from * to last st, k1.
Repeat rows 1 and 2 for a total of 8 rows, ending with a 2nd row.
Change to 4mm needles and work in st st inc 1 st at each end of every 4th row until 104(110:116) sts are reached.
Continue without further shaping until work measures (25:27:28)cm from cast-on edge.
Cast off evenly.

BUTTONBAND (right front band)

Refer to 'Tips for the Professional Finish'.
Using 3¼mm needles and with right side facing pick up 42(46:50) sts down right front opening edge.

Row 1: *k1, p1, rep from * to last st, k1.
Row 2: K2, *p1, k1, rep from * to last st, k1.
Repeat rows 1 and 2 until 10 rows have been worked. Cast off in rib, very firmly.

BUTTONHOLE BAND (left front band)

Using 3¼mm needles and starting at cast-off sts, pick up as for right side, work 4 rows rib as for right front band.

Next row: Rib 5, * cast off 2 sts, rib 13(15:17), rep from *, cast off 2 sts, rib 5.
Next row: Rib, casting on 2 sts in place of those cast off in previous row.
Rib 4 more rows and cast off firmly in rib.

COLLAR

Cast on 161(163:165) sts using 2¾mm needles.

Row 1: K2, *p1, k1, rep from * to last st, k1.
Row 2: *k1, p1, rep from * to last st, k1.
Repeat these 2 rows until work measures 5cm, change to 3¼mm needles and work a further 5cm.
Cast off firmly in rib.

POCKET TOP

Using 3¼mm needles, with right side of work facing pick up 27 sts across pocket top, work in k1 p1 rib for 8 rows. Cast off firmly in rib.

TO MAKE UP

Refer to 'Tips for the Professional Finish'.

1) Weave in all ends.
2) Block and pin and steam.
3) Join shoulder seams with an invisible seam.
4) Sew down pocket lining to inside with slip stitch.
5) Sew bottom of placket with slip stitch.
6) Sew on collar, starting at centre back, and working towards front on either side.
7) Lay work out flat and set in sleeves between armhole markers with invisible seam.
8) Sew sleeve seam with invisible stitch, sew side seams in same way allowing a 15cm vent at each side.
9) Sew on buttons.

SUMMER

Description

Sleeveless dress in 'field of wheat' stitch, can also be made as a top.

Materials

Robin Diamonte

Dress: 14(15) × 50 gram balls.

Top: 8(9) × 50 gram balls.

One pair each needles sizes 4mm and 3¼mm.

2 stitch holders.

Measurements

To fit bust
86cm–91cm   96cm–101cm

Actual measurements
102cm   111cm

Length from shoulder:Dress
110cm   112cm

Length from shoulder:Top
44cm   46cm

Additional Abbreviation

MB = make bobble (K1, yfwd, k1, yfwd, k1) in next st, turn k5, turn p5, turn k1, sl 1, k2 tog, psso, k1, turn k3 tog.

Tension

24 sts to 10cm measured over patt on size 4mm needles.

BACK AND FRONT ALIKE

With 4mm needles cast on 123(134) sts.
K3 rows.
Cont in patt as follows:

1st row: (right side) K1, * k1, MB, k2, yfwd, k1, yfwd, k4, k2 tog; rep from * to last st, k1.
2nd,4th, 6th, 8th and 10th rows: K1, * p2 tog, p10; rep from * to last st, k1.
3rd row: K1, *k5, yfwd, k1, yfwd, k3, k2 tog; rep from * to last st, k1.
5th row: K1, *k6, yfwd, k1, yfwd, k2, k2 tog; rep from * to last st, k1.
7th row: K1, * k7, (yfwd, k1) twice, k2 tog; rep from * to last st, k1.
9th row: K1, * k8, yfwd, k1, yfwd, k2 tog; rep from * to last st, k1.
11th row: K1, *sl 1, k1, psso, k4, yfwd, k1, yfwd, k2, MB, k1; rep from * to last st, k1.

12th, 14th, 16th, 18th and 20th rows:
           K1, * p10, p2 tog tbl; rep from * to last st, k1.
13th row: K1, *sl 1, k1, psso, k3, yfwd, k1, yfwd, k5; rep from * to last st, k1.
15th row: K1, *sl 1, k1, psso, k2, yfwd, k1, yfwd, k6; rep from * to last st, k1.
17th row: K1, *sl 1, k1, psso (k1, yfwd) twice, k7; rep from * to last st, k1.
19th row: K1, *sl 1, k1, psso, yfwd, k1, yfwd, k8; rep from * to last st, k1.

These 20 rows form patt.

Cont in patt until work measures 90(91)cm for Dress and 24(25)cm for Top, from cast-on edge, measured at side seams.
Mark with a contrast thread.
Work 11 more cm in patt, ending with a wrong-side row.
Shape Neck while keeping cont of patt.
Patt 46(51), leave these sts on a spare needle; patt 31(32), put these sts on to a stitch holder; patt 46(51).
Cont on the last set of sts, dec 1 st at the neck edge of the next 10(11) rows [36(40) sts].
Work straight until work measures 20(21)cm from contrast thread. Cast off.
Rejoin yarn to sts on spare needle, work to match opposite side.

NECK EDGE

First join one shoulder seam.
With 3¼mm needles and right side facing, pick up and k27 sts from open shoulder to sts on st holder, k31(32), pick up and k27 sts to shoulder seam, 27 sts to st holder, k31(32), pick up and k28 sts to open shoulder [171(173) sts].
Work 10 rows in rib.
K1 row.
Work 10 more rows in rib. Cast off loosely ribwise.

Armhole Edges (both alike)

First join the rem shoulder seam.
With 3¼mm needles and RS facing pick up and k89(93) sts evenly between the contrast threads.
Work 10 rows in rib as given for neck edge. Cast off loosely ribwise.

TO MAKE UP

Check the techniques with 'Tips for the Professional Finish'.

1) Weave in all ends.
2) With an invisible seam join sides and armhole edges.
3) Join neck band with a flat seam, turn to wrong side, slip stitch in place.

SUMMER

'ARTEMIS' – Sue

Description

Boxy top worked in cotton and ribbon using a decorative drop stitch.

Materials

Pegasus 8 ply Cotton 5(5:6) × 100 gram balls

Offray Knitting Ribbon 4(4:5) × 50 metre reels

One pair each needles sizes 6mm and 5mm.

Measurements

To fit bust
76–81cm   86–91cm   96–101cm

Actual measurements
88cm   100cm   114cm

Length from shoulder
38.5cm   40.5cm   42.5cm

Sleeve seam (approx)
18.5cm   21cm   23cm

Additional Abbreviations

A = Pegasus Cotton; B = Offray Knitting Ribbon.

Tension

15½ sts and 17½ rows to 10cm sq over the patt on size 6mm needles.

BACK AND FRONT

With 5mm needles and A, cast on 62(68:76) sts.

Work 6cm in g st.

Inc row: K6(2:10), * inc into next st, k9(6:4); rep from* to last 6(3:11) sts, inc into next st, k5(2:10) [68(78:88) sts].

Change to 6mm needles and patt.

1st and 2nd rows: With A, K 2 rows.

3rd row: (RS) With B, K7, * yrn twice, k1, yrn 3 times, k1, yrn 4 times, k1, yrn 3 times, k1, yrn twice, k6; rep from * to last st, k1.

4th row: With B, K to end letting the extra loops formed by the 'yrn' fall from needle.

5th and 6th rows: With A, K 2 rows.

7th row: With B, K2, * yrn twice, k1, yrn 3 times, k1, yrn 4 times, k1, yrn 3 times, k1, yrn twice, ** k6; rep from * to last 6 sts, rep from * to ** once more, k2.

8th row: With B, K to end letting the extra loops fall from the needle.

These 8 rows form the patt.

Cont in patt until work measures 10(12:14)cm from cast-on edge.

Mark side edges with a contrast thread.

Work a further 26cm in patt, ending with either the 4th or 8th row of patt K 7 rows in A. Cast off.

Sleeves (both alike)

With 5mm needles and A, cast on 48 sts. Work 6cm in g st.

Inc row: K4, inc into the foll 40 sts, k4 [88 sts]. Change to 6mm needles.

Cont in patt as given for Back and Front, until Sleeve measures 18.5(21:23)cm from cast-on edge, ending with either the 2nd or 6th row of patt.

Cast off with A.

TO MAKE UP

Techniques used are listed in 'Tips for the Professional Finish'.

1) Weave in ends.
2) With an invisible seam, join shoulders, leaving a space at centre for the head.
3) With an invisible seam join sleeve seams and side seams to contrast threads.
4) With an invisible seam set in sleeves.

SUMMER

DESIGN NUMBER 12
'STADIUM' – Erika

Description

Boxy shirt with button yoke and breast pocket worked in wide rib stitch.

Materials

Knitting Fever 4 ply cotton 14 × 50 gram balls

One pair needles size 3mm

3 buttons

Measurements

One size

Actual measurement
127cm

Length from shoulder
69cm

Sleeve seam
53cm

Tension

30 sts and 36 rows to 10cm sq measured over 7 × 7 rib on 3mm needles.

Stitches Used

7 × 7 rib

Row 1: * k7, p7 *, repeat.
Row 2: K the p and p the k sts of the previous row.
Repeat these rows throughout

St st (for button placket and facings)

Row 1: Knit.
Row 2: Purl.
Repeat these 2 rows.

POCKET LININGS (2 alike)

Using 3mm needles cast on 42 sts and work in st st for 15cm, leaving sts on a spare needle.

FRONT

Using 3mm needles cast on 189 sts and work in 7 × 7 rib, starting first row with purl 7, until work measures 38cm from cast-on edge.

Place pockets

With right side facing rib 35, cast off next 42 sts (in knit, not rib), rib 35, cast off next 42 sts, rib 35.
Next row: Rib as set working sts from pocket lining in place of those cast off in previous row. Continue in rib until work measures 40cm. Cast off.

BACK

Work as for front omitting the pockets.

BACK YOKE

With 3mm needles cast on 84 sts and work in 7 × 7 rib until work measures 63cm. Cast off.

FRONT YOKES

LEFT

Cast on 84 sts and work in rib, starting with purl 7, for 23cm.

Shape neck

With right side of work facing cast off 10 sts at beg of next row, then cast off 2 sts at beg of next 5 alt rows at neck edge.
Now k2 tog at neck edge of next 6 rows, (58 sts remain).

Placket

Change to st st and with right side facing work 4 rows st st.
Next row: K7, cast off 3 sts, k17, cast off 3 sts, k17, cast off 17 sts, k8.
Next row: Purl, casting on 3 sts over those cast off in previous row (to make buttonholes). Work 4 rows st st.
Next row: Purl all sts (to form ridge). Work 4 rows st st.
Repeat buttonholes so that they match when placket is folded over.
Work another 4 rows st st. Cast off.

RIGHT

Starting with knit 7 (so ribs will match at front), work as for left yoke reversing all shapings and omitting buttonholes.

SLEEVES (2 alike)

With 3mm needles cast on 84 sts and work in 7 × 7 rib for 8cm.
Keeping continuity of rib, inc 1 st at each end of next and every foll 4th row until 168 sts are reached, working extra sts into rib pattern.
Continue without further shaping until work measures 53cm.
Cast off.

TO MAKE UP

Refer to 'Tips for the Professional Finish'.

1) Weave in all ends (taking care to work on wrong side of fabric).
2) Block and pin.

3) Press work lightly (allowing rib pattern to 'flatten slightly').
4) With invisible stitch sew back yoke to back.
5) Sew pocket linings to inside of front with slip stitch.
6) Slip stitch placket facings down on front yokes and sew around buttonholes.
7) Placing left front over right front yoke, sew front yokes to front with invisible stitch.
8) With invisible stitch sew shoulder seams.
9) Open work out flat, and set in sleeves, (between markers made by yokes) with invisible stitch.
10) Using back stitch sew sleeve seams. With invisible stitch sew side seams, allowing a 15cm vent at bottom edge on each side.

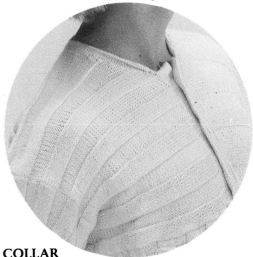

COLLAR

With right side of work facing and referring to 'Tips for the Professional Finish', with 3mm needles pick up 106 sts around neck edge as follows:
Starting at corner of right front placket pick up 36 sts up right front, 34 sts across back and 36 sts down left front
Next row: Purl
Now work 5 rows in st st. Cast off.

TO FINISH

Allow collar to roll forward.
Sew on buttons.
Turn back cuffs.

SLEEVE

RIGHT FRONT
YOKE

LEFT FRONT
YOKE

POCKET
LINING

FRONT/ BACK

SUMMER

Description

Short blouson in 'gathered stitch' with stocking stitch sleeves, saddle shoulder and zip front details, and simple-shape skirt in gathered stitch with a rib waistband.

Materials

Neveda Viscosa Cablé Cable 25(26:26) × 50gram balls

One pair each needles sizes 3¾mm and 3mm and 2¾mm

Zip 36(36:39)cm, elastic 69cm × 2.5cm wide

Measurements

Blouson

To fit bust
81–86cm   86–91cm   91–97cm

Actual measurements
91cm   97cm   102cm

Length from shoulder
44cm   46cm   51cm

Sleeve seam
39cm   41cm   42cm

Skirt

To fit hip
81–86cm   86–91cm   91–97cm

Actual width (to stretch)
79cm   84cm   89cm

Length
50cm   52cm   55cm

Tension

24 sts and 28 rows to 10cm sq measured over st st on 3¾mm needles.
22 sts and 40 rows to 10 cm sq measured over gathered st on 3¾mm and 2¾mm needles.

Stitches Used

1×1 rib
Row 1: * k1, p1.
Row 2: k the p and p the k sts of previous row.

St st
Row 1: Knit.
Row 2: Purl.
Repeat these 2 rows.

Gathered st

On 3¾mm needles work 8 rows st st, doubling the number of sts on needle on the first row by knitting twice into every st.

Change down to 2¾mm needles and work 6 rows g st (every row knit), decreasing back down to original number of sts by k2 tog across first row of 6.

BLOUSON

BACK

With 3mm needles cast on 96(102:108) sts and work in k1 p1 for 9cm.
Inc row: Rib 9(8:8), * inc into next st, rib 10(11:12), rep from * 7 times, inc into next st, rib to end [104(110:116) sts].
Change to 3¾mm needles and work in gathered st, starting with 8 rows st st as per instructions.
Continue in gathered st until work measures 20(20:23)cm from cast-on edge, 3(3:4) patt repeats.

Shape armholes

Cast off 4 sts at beg of next 2 rows, then dec 1 st at each end of next 3 foll alt rows, then dec 1 st at each end of next foll 8th rows twice [86(92:98) sts].
Continue in gathered st until a further 5 patt repeats have been worked, casting off on 6th row of g st, 38(39:41)cm approx.

LEFT FRONT

With 3mm needles cast on 50(54:58) sts and work in k1 p1 rib for 9cm, AT THE SAME TIME working a 2 st g st edge on left-hand side of needle to form an edge for the zip.
Inc row: Rib 10(10:11), * inc into next st, rib 9(10:11), rep from * 3 times, inc into next st,

work to end.
Change to 3¾mm needles and work in gathered st, keeping the 2 st garter st edge (do not include these sts in pattern).
Work in gathered st until work measures 20(20:23)cm.

Shape armhole (with RS facing)

Cast off 4 sts at beg of next row, work 1 row then dec 1 st at armhole edge on next and foll 2 alt rows, then dec 1 st on foll 8th rows twice. Continue in gathered st until work measures 36(36:39)cm from cast-on edge.

Shape neck (with WS facing)

Cast off 5 sts at beg of next row, then dec 1 st at neck edge on the following 5 rows. Cast off remaining sts.

RIGHT FRONT

Work as for left front, reversing all shapings.

SLEEVES (worked in st st)

With 3mm needles cast on 58(64:70) sts and work in k1 p1 rib for 9cm.
Inc row: Rib 8(9:10), * inc into next st, rib 7(8:9), rep from * 5 times, inc into next st, rib to end [64(70:76) sts].
Change to 3¾mm needles and st st, increasing 1 st at each end of every 3rd row until 114(120:126) sts are reached.
Continue without further shaping until work measures 39(41:42)cm.

Shape armhole

Cast off 4 sts at beg of next 2 rows, then dec 1 st at each end of next 6 rows, then cast off 2 sts at beg of every row until 30(36:42) sts remain.
Continue straight on these sts for a further 11(13:14)cm, ending with RS facing ***
Next row: k15(18:21), turn and work on these sts only for a further 9cm.
Cast off.
With RS facing rejoin yarn to remaining sts, cast off 9 sts from middle of sleeve, knit to end.
Now dec 1 st at neck edge on next and every foll alt row until all sts are worked off.
Work another sleeve to match reversing shaping at top from ***

COLLAR (worked in garter st)

With 3¾mm needles cast on 6 sts.

Row 1:   Knit 6.
Row 2:   K2, inc into next st, k to last 3 sts, inc into next st, k2.

Repeat rows 1 and 2 three times more (14 sts).

Row 9:   Knit.
Row 10:   K2, inc into next st, k to end.

Repeat rows 9 and 10 five times more (20sts).
           Work 116 rows straight on these 20 sts.

Row 137: K to last 4 sts, k2 tog, k2.
Row 138: Knit.

Repeat the last 2 rows until 14 sts remain.

Row 149: K2, k2 tog, k to last 4 sts, k2 tog, k2.
Row 150: Knit

Repeat the last 2 rows until 6 sts remain. Cast off.

TO MAKE UP

Refer to 'Tips for the Professional Finish'.
1) Weave in all ends.
2) Block and pin and steam.
3) Sew centre back yokes together with invisible seam.
4) Sew back yoke to back with invisible seam.
5) With invisible seam sew front yokes to fronts.
6) Set in sleeves around armhole.
7) Sew up sleeve seams (work from underarm to cuff) using invisible seam and sew side seams (from armhole to waist).
8) Sew on collar with slip stitch.
9) Set in zip.

RUCHED SKIRT

BACK AND FRONT (2 pieces, knitted alike)

With 2¾mm needles cast on 86(92:98) sts and work 6 rows of garter st.
Change to 3¾mm needles and work in gathered st, starting with 8 rows of st st.
Work in gathered st pattern until work measures 41(43:46)cm from cast-on edge, ending with a WS row.
Change to 3mm needles and work in k1 p1 rib for 18cm.
Cast off loosely in rib.

TO MAKE UP

Refer to 'Tips for the Professional Finish'.

1) Weave in all ends.
2) Block and pin and steam.
3) Sew up side seams with an invisible seam, take care to match pattern.
4) Refer to 'Tips for the Professional Finish' for putting in elastic (method 2).

SUMMER

Description

Cardigan in abstract patterns which can be worn with buttons at the front or back.

Materials

Scheepjeswol

MC – Linnen Brilliant 7(8) 8(9) × 50 gram balls

Linnen Brilliant White 1(1) 1(1) × 50 gram ball

Linnen Brilliant Peach 1(1) 1(1) × 50 gram ball

Fashion Lurex 2(2) 2(2) × 50 gram balls

Linnen 1(1) 1(1) × 50 gram ball

One pair each needles sizes 3¾mm and 4½mm.

5 mother of pearl buttons.

Measurements

To fit bust

81cm	86cm	91cm	96cm

Actual measurements

91cm	95cm	100cm	106cm

Length from shoulder

42cm	42cm	43cm	44cm

Sleeve seam

17cm	17cm	17cm	17cm

Tension

20 sts and 24 rows to 10cm sq measured over st st patt on size 4½mm needles.

Note

The chart pattern is worked in stocking stitch, except where indicated. Read the first and following odd-number rows (K rows) from right to left, the second and even-number rows (P rows) from left to right.

Use separate small balls of yarn for each colour motif. **Do not** strand yarn across back of work but twist strands together on wrong side when changing colour, to avoid holes.

FRONT and BACK (worked in one piece)

Front

With 3¾mm needles and MC, cast on 91(95:99:105) sts.

1st row: K1, * p1, k1; rep from * to end.

2nd row: P1, * k1, p1; rep from * to end.

Rep these 2 rows 3 times more.

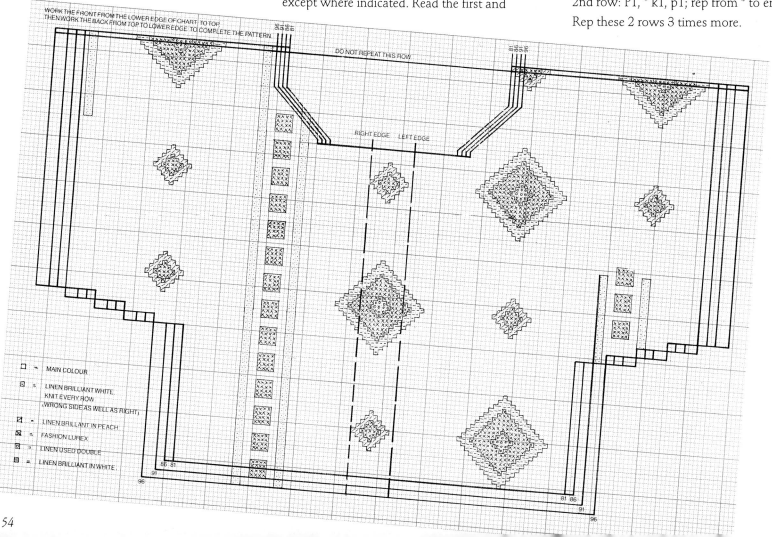

WORK THE FRONT FROM THE LOWER EDGE OF CHART TO TOP THEN WORK THE BACK FROM TOP TO LOWER EDGE TO COMPLETE THE PATTERN.

DO NOT REPEAT THIS ROW.

RIGHT EDGE   LEFT EDGE

- □ = MAIN COLOUR
- ⊞ = LINEN BRILLIANT WHITE. KNIT EVERY ROW (WRONG SIDE AS WELL AS RIGHT)
- ◪ = LINEN BRILLIANT IN PEACH
- ⊠ = FASHION LUREX
- ⊙ = LINEN USED DOUBLE
- ⊟ = LINEN BRILLIANT IN WHITE

Change to 4½mm needles and p1 row, inc 1 st in middle of the row [92(96:100:106)sts]. Cont to work in patt from chart. Work 30(30:32:34) rows.

Shape sleeves

Cast on and work into chart patt 7 sts at the beg of the next 8 rows [148(152:156:162) sts]. Work 37 more rows in chart patt.

Shape neck

Whilst keeping chart patt correct, patt 59(60:61:63) sts and turn, leaving the rem sts on a spare needle. Cont on this first set of sts for left side of neck.

** Dec 1 st at neck edge on the next 11 rows [48(49:50:52) sts].
Work 9 rows straight. Mark each end of last row with a contrasting marker thread, to indicate shoulder.

To work left back

Cont to read the chart from top to bottom, beg with the 2nd row from the top and reading it from left to right.
Work 8 more rows from chart.

Shape back neck

Inc and work into chart patt 1 st at the neck edge on the next 11 rows [59(60:61:63) sts].
Work 1 row straight. (Do not work this row for right back.)
Cast on 10(11:12:13) sts at the beg of the next row [69(71:73:76) sts].
Work 36 rows straight.

Shape sleeve

Cast off 7 sts at beg of next and foll 3 alt rows [41(43:45:48) sts].
Work 30(30:32:34) rows straight.

Next row: P to end, dec 1 st in centre for the 4th size only [41(43:45:47)sts].
Change to 3¾mm needles.
Work 8 rows in rib as given for front welt. Cast off loosely ribwise.

To work right side of neck

Return to sts on spare needle and place 30(32:34:36) centre front sts onto a holder.
With RS facing, join in yarn to rem sts at neck edge and patt to end. Complete as for left side from **, noting the bracketed exception.

NECK BAND

With RS facing, using 3¾mm needles and MC pick up and k10(11:12:13) sts along cast-on sts of left back neck, 37 sts round neck edge to centre front sts, k30(32:34:36) sts from holder, pick up and k36 sts round neck to cast on sts of right back neck, then 10(11:12:13) sts along cast-on edge [125(129:133:137) sts].
Work 8 rows in rib as given for front welt. Cast off ribwise.

BUTTONHOLE BAND

With RS facing, using 3¾mm needles and MC, pick up and k75(75:77:79) sts evenly along left back edge.
Work 5 rows in rib as given for welt, beg with a 2nd row.

1st buttonhole row: Rib 4(4:5:6), * cast off the next 3 sts, rib 13 including the st used in casting off; rep from * 3 times more, cast off the next 3 sts, rib to end.

2nd buttonhole row: Rib 4(4:5:6), * cast on 3 sts, rib 13; rep from * 3 times more, cast on 3 sts, rib to end.
Work 5 rows in rib. Cast off ribwise.

BUTTON BAND

With RS facing, using 3¾mm needles and MC, pick up and k75(75:77:79) sts down right back edge. Work 12 rows in rib. Cast off ribwise.

CUFFS

With RS facing, using 3¾mm needles and MC, pick up and k85(89:91:95) sts, evenly along each cuff edge. Work 8 rows in rib. Cast off ribwise.

TO MAKE UP

Techniques used are listed in 'Tips for the Professional Finish'.
1) Weave in ends.

2) With an invisible seam, join sides and underarms.
3) Sew buttons onto buttonband.

'BALI'

KNITTING STANDARD

Description

Skinny rib vest with 'keyhole back'.

Materials

Scheepjes Linnen 6(7:8) × 50 gram balls

One pair each circular needles sizes 3¼mm, 2¾mm and 2¼mm

One small button

Measurements

To fit bust
81–86cm   86–91cm   91–96cm

Length from shoulder
75cm   79cm   81cm

Tension

38 sts and 34 rows to 10cm sq measured flat over rib on size 3¼mm needles.

NB This garment is made in one piece.

With a 3¼mm circular needle cast on 240(256:272) sts.
Work in rounds of k1 p1 rib until the top measures 24(25:26)cm.
Mark with a contrast thread.
Change to a 2¾mm needle.
Cont in rib for a further 12cm.
Change to a 2¼mm needle.
Cont in rib until the top measures 20cm from contrast thread.
Change to a 3¼mm needle.
Cont in rib until the top measures 26(27:28)cm from contrast thread.

Divide for Left Back while keeping the cont of rib.

Dec first st of the next round, rib 238(254:270).
Cont in rib but now work to and fro across the needle, NOT IN ROUNDS.
Work 4(6:8) rows, ending with a wrong side row.

Shape Armhole while keeping the cont of rib.

Rib 55(59:63), turn, leaving the rem sts on a spare needle.
Cast off 4 sts at the beg of the next row, work one row straight.
Dec 1 st at (beg) the armhole edge of the next

and every foll alt row until 30(32:34) sts rem.
Work 8(2:0) rows straight.

Shape Back Neck while keeping the cont of rib.

Rib 13, put these sts onto a st holder, rib to end of row.
Cont in rib dec 1 st at the neck edge of the next 11(12:13) rows [6(7:8) sts].
Work 15(17:17) rows. Cast off.
Rejoin the yarn to sts on spare needle, with right side of work facing.

Shape Front Armholes while keeping the cont of rib.

Rib 3, rib 2 tog, rib 3, put these sts onto a safety pin, rib 113(121:129), turn, leaving the rem sts on a spare needle.
Work one row.
Cast off 4 sts at the beg of the next 2 rows.
Dec 1 st at each end of the next and every foll alt row until 63(67:71) sts rem.
Work 9(3:1) rows.

Shape Neck while keeping the cont of rib.

Rib 17(19:21), turn leaving the rem sts on a spare needle.
Cont on the first sts dec 1 st at the neck edge of the next 11(12:13) rows [6(7:8) sts].
Work 15(17:17) rows. Cast off.
Rejoin the yarn to sts on spare needle, with right side of work facing.
Rib 29, put these sts onto a st holder, rib to end.
Work the rem sts to match the opposite side.

RIGHT BACK

Rejoin the yarn to rem sts.
Next row: rib 3, rib 2 tog, rib 3, put these sts onto a safety pin, rib to end.
Work the rem 55(59:63) sts to match the opposite side remembering to reverse the shapings.

Armhole Edges (both alike)

With 2¼mm needles and RS facing pick up and k75(79:81) sts from open shoulder to 7 sts on safety pin, rib 7, marking the centre st with a contrast thread, pick up and k75(79:81) sts along the opposite edge.
Work 8 rows in rib dec 1 st either side of centre st on every alt row.
Cast off ribwise.

Neck Edge

First join both shoulder seams.
With a 2¼mm needle cast on 9 sts, rib 13 sts of left back neck, pick up and k29 sts to shoulder, 28 sts down front neck edge to sts on st holder, rib 29, pick up and k28 sts to right shoulder

seam, 29 sts to sts of back neck, rib 13, cast on 13.
Work 3 rows in rib.

Buttonhole

1st row: rib 4, cast off 3, rib to end of row.
2nd row: rib to last 4 sts, cast on 3, rib 4.

Work 3 more rows in rib. Cast off ribwise.

TO FINISH

1) Weave in all ends.
2) Sew button to back.

SUMMER

'MIRAGE' – Sue

Description

Cutaway, top in cables, with buttoned collar and 'keyhole' back over ribbed skirt.

Materials

Richard Poppleton Sorrento DK.

Top

5(5:6:7) × 50 gram balls

Skirt

10(11:12:13) × 50 gram balls

One pair each of 3¼mm and 4mm knitting needles.
1 cable needle
1 circular needle sizes 3¾mm, 3¼mm and 2¾mm for skirt.
2 mother of pearl buttons.
Elastic 5cm wide to fit waist.

Measurements

Top

To fit bust

81cm	86cm	91cm	96cm

Actual measurements

87cm	92cm	97cm	102cm

Length from shoulder

35cm	36cm	37cm	38cm

Skirt

To fit hips

86cm	91cm	96cm	101cm

Additional Abbreviation: Cr6 = cross 6, sl 3 sts onto a cn, hold at front of work, k3, k sts on cn.

Tension

22sts and 28 rows to 10cm sq measured over st st on size 4mm needles.

FRONT

With 3¼mm needles cast on 101(107:113:119) sts.

1st row: K1, p1 to last st, k1.
2nd row: P1, k1 to last st, p1.
These two rows form rib, rep 1st and 2nd rows twice, then 1st row again.

Inc row: Rib 10(13:16:19), * inc in next st, rib 9, rep from * ending row rib 10(13:16:19) [110(116:124:130) sts].
Change to 4mm needles.

1st row: (right side) k1, p1(4:7:10), * k1, p4, k6, p4; rep from * to last 3(6:9:12) sts, k1, p1(4:7:10), k1.
2nd row: K2(5:8:11), * p1, k4, p6, k4; rep from * to last 3(6:9:12) sts, p1, k2(5:8:11).
3rd row: K1, p1(4:7:10), * k1, p4, Cr6, p4; rep from * to last 3(6:9:12) sts, k1, p1(4:7:10), k1.
4th row: as 2nd
5th to 8th rows: as 1st and 2nd.
These 8 rows form patt.
Cont in patt until front measures 14(15:16:17)cm from cast-on edge, ending with a WS row.

Shape Armholes while keeping cont of patt.
Cast off 4 sts at the beg of the next 4 rows **
Dec 1 st at each end of next and every foll alt rows until 74(74:76:78) sts rem.
Work 19(13:9:5) rows straight.

Shape Neck while keeping cont of patt.
Patt 25(25:26:27), turn leaving rem sts on a spare needle.
Cont on first sts dec 1 st at the neck edge of the foll 10(10:11:12) rows [15 sts].
Work straight until front measures 23(24:24:25)cm from beg of armhole shaping. Cast off.
Rejoin yarn to sts on spare needle.
Cast off 9, k6, put these sts on a safety pin,

cast off 9, patt to end.
Work rem sts to match opposite side.

BACK

Work as front to **
Divide Back while keeping cont of patt.
Dec 1, patt 42(45:49:52), turn leaving rem sts on a spare needle.
Cont on first sts dec 1 st at the armhole edge of every foll RS row until 34(34:35:36) sts rem.
Work straight until back matches front. Cast off.
Rejoin yarn to sts on spare needle.
* k3, put these sts on a safety pin, rep from * once, patt to end dec last st.
Work rem sts to match opposite side.

Back Edges (both alike)
Put 3 sts onto 3¼mm needles, making 1st row RS cont in rib until band matches edge, return sts to safety pin.

Collar (all sizes). First join both shoulder seams.

With 3¼mm needles rib 3 sts of left back edge, pick up and k16 sts across left back neck, 19 sts down left front edge to cast-off sts, 7 sts to sts on safety pin, k6, pick up and k7 sts across cast-off sts, 19 sts to shoulder and 16 sts across right back neck, rib 3 [96 sts].

1st row: (wrong side) rib 3, k6, * p6, k6; rep from * to last 3 sts, rib 3.
2nd row: Rib 3, p6, * Cr6, p6; rep from * to last 3 sts, rib 3.
3rd row: as 1st.
4th row: Rib 3, p6, * k6, p6, rep from * to last 3 sts, rib 3.
5th to 8th rows: as 1st and 4th.
Rep 1st to 8th rows once then 1st to 4th rows again.

Dec row: Rib 3, cont working in rib as follows: rib 4 *, rib 2 tog, rib 6; rep from * to last 9 sts, rib 2 tog, rib to end [85 sts].
Work 4 rows in rib. Cast off ribwise.

Armhole Edges (both alike)

With 3¼mm needles and RS facing pick up and k105(107:109:111) sts evenly round edge.
Work 8 rows in rib dec 1st at each end of every alt row.
Cast off ribwise.

TO MAKE UP

All the techniques are listed in 'Tips for the Professional Finish'.

1) Weave in all ends.
2) With an invisible seam sew bands into place.
3) With an invisible seam join sides.
4) Make 2 button loops along right collar edge, sew buttons onto left edge.

SKIRT is worked in one piece.

With 3¾mm needles cast on 229(241:253:265) sts.

1st row: Work across needle not in rounds. K1, p1, to last st, k1.
2nd row: (wrong side) p1, k1, to last st, p1.
Rep these 2 rows until the skirt measures 18cm ending with a wrong side row.

Next row: K1, p1 to last st, leave this st on needle. DO NOT TURN.
Next row is worked in round: k2 tog (last st of previous row and first st of this), rib to end.
Cont in rib but now work in rounds until the skirt measures 60(60:61:62)cm.
Change to a 3¼mm needle, cont in rib until the skirt measures 68(68:69:70)cm.
Change to a 2¾mm needle, cont in rib until the skirt measures 78(79:80:81)cm.
Cast off ribwise.

TO COMPLETE

All the techniques are listed in 'Tips for the Professional Finish'.

1) Weave in all ends.
2) Make a herringbone casing over the elastic.

SUMMER

Description

One of Erika's favourite patterns from the 1950s – a loose, raglan-sleeve sweater, with stitch pattern yoke, zip front and roll collar details.

Materials

Neveda 4 ply Cotton 10(10:11) × 50 gram balls

Neveda 4 ply Cotton 10(10:11) × 50 gram balls

One pair each needles sizes 2¾mm and 3¼mm and stitch holder.

25cm zip

Measurements

To fit chest
91–97cm   97–102cm   102–107cm

Actual measurements
107cm   112cm   117cm

Length from shoulder
69cm   70cm   71cm

Sleeve seam
46cm   48cm   48cm

Additional Abbreviations

TW2f = knit second st from front, knit first st, slip sts off needle tog.
TW2b = knit into back of second st, knit into first st, slip sts off needle tog.

Tension

26 sts and 34 rows to 10cm sq measured over st st on 3¼mm needles.

BACK

Using 2¾mm needles cast on 142(148:154) sts and work in k1 p1 rib for 8cm.
Change to 3¼mm needles and work in st st until work measures 38(38:39)cm from cast-on edge, ending with a purl row.

Shape raglan

Row 1:   K2, sl 1, k1, psso, knit to last 4 sts, k2 tog, k2.
Row 2:   Purl.
Repeat these 2 rows until 40(42:44) sts remain, leaving sts on a holder.

FRONT

Work as for back until work measures 37(37:38)cm, ending with a purl row.

Divide for yoke

Row 1:   K68(71:74) sts, sl 1, k2 tog, psso, turn, work on this group of sts only.
Row 2:   Purl.
Row 3:   K to last 3 sts, sl 1, k2 tog, psso.
Row 4:   Purl.
Row 5:   K2, sl 1, k1, psso, knit to last 3 sts, sl 1, k2 tog, psso.
Repeat the last 2 rows until 4 sts remain.
Next row: K2, sl 1, k1, psso. Cast off these 3 sts.
With right side of work facing return to remaining sts of yoke.

Row 1:   Knit.
Row 2:   Purl to last 3 sts, sl 1, p2 tog, psso.
Repeat the last 2 rows once more.

Row 5:   Knit to last 4 sts, k2 tog, k2.
Row 6:   Purl to last 3 sts, sl 1, p2 tog, psso.
Repeat the last 2 rows until 4 sts are left.
Next row: P1, sl 1, p2 tog, psso. Cast off these 2 sts.

LEFT SLEEVE

With 2¾mm needles cast on 78(82:86) sts and work in k 1 p1 rib for 9cm.
Change to 3¼mm needles and work in st st increasing 1 st at each end of next and every foll 3rd row until 134(142:150) sts are reached. Continue straight until work mesures 46(48:48)cm from cast-on edge, ending with a purl row.

Shape sleeve head

Row 1:   K2, sl 1, k1, psso, knit to last 4 sts, k2 tog, k2.
Row 2:   Purl.
Repeat the last 2 rows until 86(90:94) sts remain, ending with a purl row.
Next row: K2, sl 1, k1, psso k39(41:43), slip remaining 43(45:47) sts onto a st holder and continue to work on the first group of sts, dec 1 st at beg of every alt row as before and keeping centre edge straight until 16(18:20) sts remain. Slip these sts onto a st holder.

RIGHT SLEEVE

Work as given for left sleeve until 86(90:94) sts remain, ending with a knit row.
Next row: P43(45:47), turn, slip remaining 43(45:47) sts onto a holder and work on first group only, dec 1 st at end of the next and every foll alt row as before until 16(18:20) sts remain, slip sts onto holder.
Tack firmly together the short edges of raglan sleeves to each side of front and long edges of sleeve to back.

LEFT YOKE

With right side of work facing and 2¾mm needles commence at centre of left sleeve and k43(45:47) sts from st holder, then pick up and knit 70(74:78) sts along front to centre 'V' [113(119:125) sts].
Work yoke pattern as follows:

NB When slipping a st throughout yoke, bring wool forward, sl st purlwise, then put wool back before knitting next stitch.

Row 1: (wrong side) K2, * sl 1 pwise, k2, rep from * to end of row.

Row 2: K2, *TW2b (k into back of 2nd st, k into first st, slip sts off needle tog), k1, rep from * to last 3 sts, k1, k2 tog.

Row 3: * sl 1 pwise, k2, rep from * to last st, sl 1 pwise

Row 4: * TW2b, k1, rep from * to last 4 sts, TW2b, k2 tog

Row 5: * k1, sl 1 pwise, k1, rep from * to end

Row 6: * k1, TW2b, rep from * to last 3 sts, k1, k2 tog.

Row 7: * k2, sl 1 pwise, rep from * to last 2 sts, k2.

Row 8: K2, * TW2b, k1, rep from * to last 3 sts, k1, k2 tog

Row 9: * sl 1 pwise, k2, rep from * to last st, k1.

Row 10: K2, * TW2f (k 2nd st from front, k first st, slip sts off needle tog), k1, rep from * to last 2 sts, k2 tog.

Row 11: * sl 1 pwise, k2, rep from * to end of row.

Row 12: * k1, TW2f, rep from * to last 3 sts, k1, k2 tog.

Row 13: * sl 1 pwise, k2, rep from * to last 2 sts, sl 1 k1.

Row 14: * TW2f, k1, rep from * to last 2 sts, k2 tog.

Row 15: * sl 1 pwise, k2, rep from * to last st, k1.

Row 16: K2, * TW2f, k1, rep from * to last 2 sts, k2 tog.

Row 17: * sl 1 pwise, k2, rep from * to end.

Row 18: K2 tog, k to the last 2 sts, k2 tog.

Row 19: * k2, sl 1 pwise, rep from * to last st, k1.

Row 20: As 18th row.

Row 21: * k1, sl 1 pwise, k1, rep from * to last 2 sts, k1, sl 1.

Row 22: As 18th row.

Repeat the last 6 rows twice more, then work rows 17 to 21.

Row 40: K2 tog, * k1, TW2b, rep from * to last 3 sts, k1, k2 tog.

Row 41: * K2, sl 1 pwise, rep from * to end.

Row 42: K2 tog, * k1, TW2b, rep from * to last 4 sts, k2, k2 tog.

Row 43: * sl 1 pwise, k2, rep from * to last st, k1.

Row 44: K2 tog, * k1, TW2b, rep from * to last 2 sts, k2 tog.

Row 45: * k1, sl 1 pwise, k1, rep from * to last 2 sts, sl 1, k1.

Row 46: K2 tog, * k1, TW2b, rep from * to last 3 sts, k1, k2 tog.

Row 47: As 41st row

Row 48: K2 tog, *TW2f, k1, rep from * to last 4 sts, TW2f, k2 tog.

Row 49: * k2, sl 1 pwise, rep from * to last st, k1.

Row 50: K2 tog, * k1, TW2f, rep from * to last 2 sts, k2 tog.

Row 51: K2, * sl 1 pwise, k2, rep from * to end.

Row 52: K2 tog, k2, *TW2f, k1, rep from * to last 4 sts, TW2f, k2 tog.

Row 53: * K2, sl1 pwise, rep from * to end.

Row 54: K2 tog, *TW2f, k1, rep from * to last 4 sts, TW2f, k2 tog

Row 55: * k2, sl 1 pwise, rep from * to last st, k1.

Row 56: K2 tog, k to last 2 sts, k2 tog.

Row 57: K1, * sl 1 pwise, k2, rep from * to last st, k1.

Row 58: as 56th row

Continue, keeping ribs straight, working right-side rows as row 56, and wrong-side rows with a sl st over the smooth rib and k2 in between until 35(37:39) sts remain, ending with a row on the wrong side of work.
Slip these sts onto a st holder.

Right Yoke

With right side of work facing and 2¾mm needles commence at centre front and pick up and knit 70(74:78) sts to right sleeve, then knit 43(45:47) sts left from right sleeve [113(119:125) sts].

Work in pattern as follows:

Row 1: (wrong side), * k2, sl 1 pwise, rep from * to last 2 sts, k2.

Row 2: K2 tog, k1, * k1, TW2f, rep from * to last 2 sts, k2.

Row 3: * sl 1 pwise, k2, rep from * to last st, sl 1.

Row 4: K2 tog, *TW2f, k1, rep from * to last 2 sts, TW2f.

Row 5: * k1, sl 1 pwise, k1, rep from * to end.

Row 6: k2 tog, * k1, TW2f, rep from * to last st, k1.

Row 7: * k2, sl 1 pwise, rep from * to last 2 sts, k2.

Row 8: K2 tog, k1, * k1, TW2f, rep from * to last 2 sts, k2.

Row 9: * sl 1 pwise, k2, rep from * to last st, sl 1.

Row 10: K2 tog, * k1, TW2b, rep from * to last 2 sts, k2.

Row 11: * k2, sl 1 pwise, rep from * to end.

Row 12: K2 tog, * k1, TW2b, rep from * to last st, k1.

Row 13: * k1, sl 1 pwise, k1, rep from * to last 2 sts, k1, sl 1.

Row 14: K2 tog, * k1, TW2b, rep from * to end.

Row 15: * sl 1 pwise, k2, rep from * to last st, sl 1.

Row 16: K2 tog, * k1, TW2b, rep from * to last 2 sts, k2.

Row 17: * k2, sl 1 pwise, rep from * to end.

Row 18: K2 tog, k to last 2 sts, k2 tog.

Row 19: * k1, sl 1 pwise, k1, rep from * to last st, k1.

Row 20: As 18th row

Row 21: * sl 1 pwise, k2, rep from * to last 2 sts, sl 1, k1.

Row 22: As 18th row.

Repeat the last 6 rows twice more, then repeat rows 17 to 21

Row 40: K2 tog, * k1, TW2f, rep from * to last 3 sts, k1, k2 tog.

Row 41: * sl 1 pwise, k2, rep from * to end.

Row 42: K2 tog, k1, * k1, TW2f, rep from * to last 3 sts, k1, k2 tog.

Row 43: * sl 1 pwise, k2, rep from * to last st sl1.

Row 44: K2 tog, *TW2f, k1, rep from * to last 2 sts, k2 tog.

Row 45: * sl 1 pwise, k2, rep from * to last 2 sts, sl 1, k1.

Row 46: K2 tog, * k1, TW2f, rep from * to last 3 sts, k1, k2 tog.

Row 47: * sl 1 pwise, k2, rep from * to end.

Row 48: K2 tog, *TW2b, k1, rep from * to last 4 sts, TW2b, k2 tog.

Row 49: * k1, sl 1 pwise, k1, rep from * to last st, k1.

Row 50: K2 tog, *TW2b, k1, rep from * to last 2 sts, k2 tog.

Row 51: * K2, sl 1 pwise, rep from * to last 2 sts, k2.

Row 52: K2 tog, *TW2b, k1, rep from * to last 3 sts, k1, k2 tog.

Row 53: * sl 1 pwise, k2, rep from * to end.

Row 54: K2 tog, *TW2b, k1, rep from * to last 4 sts, TW2b, k2 tog.

Row 55: * k1, sl 1 pwise, k1, rep from * to last st, k1.

Row 56: K2 tog, k to last 2 sts, k2 tog.

Continue keeping ribs straight and dec 1 st at each end of every alt row as instructions for left yoke until 35(37:39) sts remain, ending at front edge.

NECKBAND

Now arrange all sts on one needle, i.e. left yoke 35(37:39) sts, 16(18:20) sts from top of left sleeve, 40(42:44) sts from back, 16(18:20) sts from top of right sleeve, 35(37:39) sts from right yoke, a total of 142(152:162) sts on needle.
Now work in pattern across all sts for 13cm, straight ribs (dec 1 st at top of right sleeve if necessary to bring new sts into pattern).
Cast off loosely.

TO MAKE UP

Refer to 'Tips for the Professional Finish'.

1) Weave in all ends.
2) Block and pin.
3) Steam.
4) Fold collar to inside to form a double band of 6cm and slip stitch around inside of neck (leaving front edges open).
5) Sew in zip (referring to 'Tips for the Professional Finish') taking note to slip the top (6cm) of the zip tapes between collar opening. Sew down firmly, close to zip.
6) With an invisible seam sew raglan shoulders.
7) With an invisible seam sew side and sleeve seams.

AUTUMN

"Season of mists and mellow fruitfulness,
Close bosom-friend of the maturing sun."

John Keats

Lurex yarn adds textural impact!

Leather thonging

Mélange yarns
create surface interest...

experiment
with colour
combinations

65

AUTUMN

DESIGN NUMBER 17
'CATHY' – Sue

THE PATTERNS

KNITTING STANDARD ✗✗✗

Description

Top in cables with jacquard bands and shawl collar.

Materials

Kilcara Cottage

MC – Main col Red 16(18:20) × 50 gram balls

A – 1st contrast col yellow 4(5:6) × 50 gram balls

B – 2nd contrast col purple 8(9:10) × 50 gram balls

One pair each needles sizes 5½mm, 5mm and 6mm. 5½mm circular needle for the collar.

1 cable needle

Measurements

To fit bust
81–86cm   91–96cm   101–106cm

Actual measurements
98cm   105cm   112cm

Length from shoulder
76cm   77cm   78cm

Sleeve seam (approx)
50cm   50cm   50cm

Additional abbreviation: CR6 = sl the next 3 sts onto cable needle, K3, K sts on the cable needle.

Tension

17 sts and 18 rows to 10 cm sq measured over st st on size 5½mm needles.

BACK

With 5mm needles and MC, cast on 97(103:109) sts.

1st row: k1 p1 to last st, k1.

2nd row: p1 k1 to last st, p1.

These 2 rows form rib, rep 1st and 2nd rows 3 more times inc 1 st at the end of last row [98(104:110) sts].

Change to 6mm needles.

1st row: (right side) k1, p3(6:9), k6, *p6, k6; rep from * to last 4(7:10) sts, p3(6:9), k1.

2nd row: k4(7:10), p6, *k6, p6; rep from * to last 4(7:10) sts, k to end.

3rd row: k1, p3(6:9), CR6, *p6, CR6; rep from * to last 4(7:10) sts, p3(6:9), k1.

4th row: as 2nd.

5th to 8th rows: as 1st and 2nd.

These 8 rows form cable patt.

Rep 1st to 8th rows 4 more times then 1st to 4th rows again.

Change to A and 5½mm needles.

Next row: k6(9:12), *k2 tog, k4; rep from * to last 2(5:8) sts, k to end [83(89:95) sts].

k3 rows with A.

Beg with a K row cont in st st foll patt set on chart for 34 rows.

k4 rows with A.

Change to 6mm needles and MC **

Next row: k6(9:12), * inc in next st, k4; rep from * to last 2(5:8) sts, k to end [98(104:110) sts].

Beg with 2nd row, cont in cable patt until the back measures 71(72:73)cm, from cast-on edge, ending with a WS row.

Shape neck while keeping cont of patt.

Patt 31(33:35), turn, leaving rem sts on a spare needle.

Cont on first sts dec 1 st at the neck edge of the foll 7(7:6) rows.

Work 2(2:3) rows straight.

Cast off rem 24(26:29) sts.

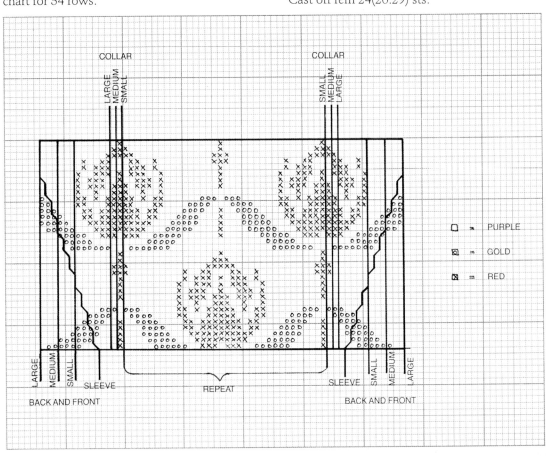

COLLAR

LARGE MEDIUM SMALL

SMALL MEDIUM LARGE

□ = PURPLE

⬚ = GOLD

⬚ = RED

LARGE MEDIUM SMALL

SLEEVE

REPEAT

SLEEVE

SMALL MEDIUM LARGE

BACK AND FRONT

BACK AND FRONT

Rejoin yarn to sts on spare needle.

Cast off 36(38:40), patt to end.

Work the rem 31(33:35) sts to match the opposite side.

FRONT

Work as back to **

Next row: k6(9:12), inc in next st, (k4, inc in next st) 3 times, k2 [28(31:34) sts], turn, leaving rem sts on a spare needle.

Foll row: k6, p6, k6, p6, k4(7:10).

This row sets cable patt.

Cont in patt dec 1 st at the neck edge of every 4th row until 24(26:29) sts rem. Work straight until the front matches back. Cast off.

Rejoin A to sts on spare needle, cast off 35 sts, change to MC, k2, (inc in next st, k4) 3 times, inc in next st, k6(9:12) [28(31:34) sts].

Foll row: k4(7:10), p6, k6, p6, k6.

This row sets cable patt.

Work to match the opposite side.

SLEEVES (both alike, all sizes)

With 5mm needles and MC, cast on 37 sts.

Work 21 rows in rib.

Next row: inc in every st [74 sts].

Change to 6mm needles.

Cont in patt as set for back, foll first set of figures for 20 rows.

AT THE SAME TIME SHAPE SLEEVE (while keeping cont of patt) by inc 1 st at each end of 2nd and every foll 3rd row [88 sts].

Change to 5½mm needles and A.

Next row: k7, *k2 tog, k4; rep from * to last 3 sts, k3 [75 sts].

K3 rows with A.

Beg with K row cont in st st foll patt set on chart and cont inc on every 3rd row for 27 rows [93 sts]. Complete chart working straight.

Change to A, k4 rows.

Change to 6mm needles and MC.

Next row: k6, * inc in next st, k4; rep from * to last 2 sts, k2 [110 sts].

Beg with 2nd row cont in cable patt foll 3rd set of figures for 19 rows. Cast off.

COLLAR

First join both shoulder seams.

With a 5½mm circular needle, A and right side facing pick up and k136(138:140) sts evenly round neck edge, omitting cast-off sts of front neck.

Work to and fro across needle as follows:

With A, k3 rows.

Cont in st st foll 34 rows of patt set on chart.

With A, k4 rows.

Beg with K row work 4 rows st st.

Cast off.

TO MAKE UP

All required techniques are listed in 'Tips for the Professional Finish'.

1) Weave in all ends.
2) Fold 4 rows of collar in st st to WS, slip stitch in place. Overlap left over right and stitch to cast-off stitches of front neck, with an invisible seam.
3) With invisible seam sew sleeve seams and then side seams to end of colour pattern.
4) With a back stitch sew in sleeves.

AUTUMN

Description

Long, oversize, 'V' neck cardigan coat in 'plaid or tartan' design, with deep pockets and big button details.

Materials

Argyll Finesse Mohair

A – Black 21 × 25 gram balls

B – Yellow 14 × 25 gram balls

C – Red 7 × 25 gram balls

D – Green 2 × 25 gram balls

One pair each needles sizes 4mm and 5mm (long), 4mm circular needle and stitch holder, spare needles.

3 large ornamental buttons.

Measurements

One size

Actual measurements
132cm

Length from shoulder
99cm

Sleeve seam
46cm

Tension

20 sts and 19 rows to 10cm sq measured over 'tartan' pattern on 5mm needles.

NB Pattern uses 'stranding or Fair Isle technique' from a chart.

Special Note

'Stranding or Fair Isle technique' is used on chart for colours A and B. Colours C and D can be knitted into pattern or 'Swiss darned' on afterwards.

BACK

Using 4mm needles and C cast on 136 sts and work in k2 p2 rib for 8cm.
Change to 5mm and st st and follow tartan or plaid pattern from chart until work measures 65cm from cast-on edge.

Mark each end of next row with a coloured thread to indicate armhole position.
Continue straight in tartan/plaid pattern until work measures 94cm.

Shape shoulders by casting off 16 sts at beg of next 6 rows.

Work 1 row and leave remaining 40 sts on a st holder.

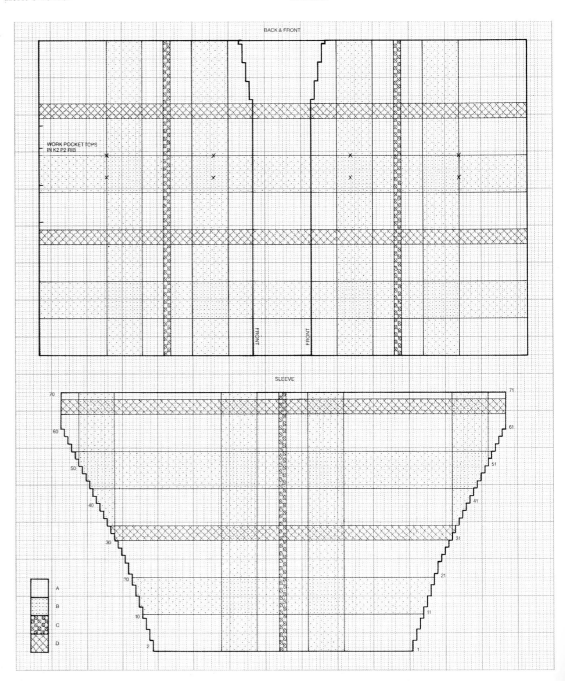

POCKET LININGS (2)

With 5mm needles and A cast on 30 sts and work in st st for 18cm, leaving sts on a spare needle.

RIGHT FRONT

With 4mm needles and C cast on 60 sts and work in k2 p2 for 8cm.

Change to 5mm needles and work in tartan/plaid pattern until work measures 36cm from cast-on edge.

Whilst keeping to tartan/plaid pattern place pocket top between markers on chart as follows:

K11 in patt, k2 p2 in C for 30 sts, patt to end.

Continue to work 30 sts in k2 p2 rib for pocket top for a total of 5 rows and cast off the 30 sts in rib on the 6th row.

Next row: K11 in patt, k in patt placing 30 sts of pocket lining in place of those cast off in previous row, patt to end.

Continue straight in tartan/plaid pattern until work measures 46cm.

Shape neck by dec 1 st at neck edge on next and every foll 5th row until 48 sts remain.

When work measures 65cm place a coloured thread at side edge to mark armhole position.

Continue on 48 sts until work measures 94cm and cast off shoulders to match back.

LEFT FRONT

Work as for right front reversing all shaping.

SLEEVES (2 alike)

With 4mm needles and C cast on 72 sts and work in k2 p2 rib for 8cm.

Change to 5mm needles and work in tartan/plaid pattern AT THE SAME TIME inc 1 st at each end of every 3rd row until 88 sts are reached, then inc 1 st at each end of every alt row until 124 sts are reached, bringing all extra sts into the tartan pattern.

Continue straight until work measures 46cm.
Cast off.

BUTTONBAND

Referring to 'Tips for the Professional Finish' join shoulder seams with an invisible seam.

Using 4mm long or circular needle and C, with right side facing pick up and knit 175 sts evenly up right front, 40 sts from st holder, 175 sts down left front (390 sts).

Work back and forth in k2 p2 rib for approx 3cm, ending at bottom of right front.

Place 3 buttonholes up right front as follows:
Rib for 8cm, cast off 4 sts, * rib for 15cm, cast off 4 sts, repeat from * once more, continue in rib to end of row.

Next row: Rib, casting on 4 sts in place of those cast off in previous row.
Continue in rib until band measures 7cm. Cast off.

TO MAKE UP

Refer to 'Tips for the Professional Finish'.

1) Weave in all ends.
2) Block and pin and steam.
3) Lay work out flat and set in sleeves between armhole markers with invisible seams.
4) Sew sleeve and side seams.
5) Slip stitch pocket linings into position on inside.
6) Sew on buttons.

'ARGYLL LEGGINGS'

KNITTING STANDARD ✗ ✗ ✗

Description

Leggings in fine tweed yarns, with Argyll pattern detail and elasticated waistband.

Materials

Rowan Fine Nep Tweed

MC – Black 4 × 50 gram balls

1st C – Red 2 × 50 gram balls

2nd C – Purple 2 × 50 gram balls

3rd C – Gold 1 × 50 gram ball

One pair each needles sizes 3¼mm and 2¾mm.

Elastic 6cm wide to fit waist

Measurements

One size

Inside leg seam
61cm

Tension

32 sts and 40 rows to 10cm sq measured over st st on 3¼mm needles.

NB Pattern uses colour block method and small chart for pattern.

LEFT LEG

With 2¾mm needles and MC cast on 70 sts and work in k1 p1 rib for 13cm.
Change to 3¼mm needles and work in st st, referring to chart as given for Argyll motif, placing pattern as follows:

Row 1: (with right side facing) k20 MC, k1 3rd C, k13 MC, k2 1st C, k13 MC, k1 3rd C, k20 MC.
Continue in st st working pattern as now set whilst inc 1 st at each end of every 4th row until 88 sts are reached.
Continue without further shaping for 13cm.
Now inc 1 st at each end of next and every foll 4th row until 144 sts are reached, whilst continuing to work Argyll motif up centre of work.
Mark each end of last row with a coloured thread to indicate top of leg seam. ***
Work 53 rows without shaping.
Next row: (with wrong side facing) p2 tog, p to end of row.
Dec this way on every foll 4th row until 133 sts remain.
Shape for back as follows:
Row 1: K1, k2 tog, k56, TURN.
Row 2 and alt rows: Purl.

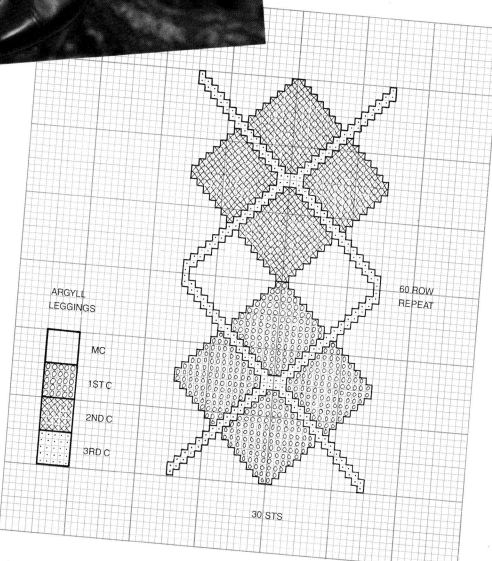

ARGYLL
LEGGINGS

MC

1ST C

2ND C

3RD C

60 ROW
REPEAT

30 STS

Row 3: k54, TURN.
Row 5: k1, k2 tog, k47, TURN.
Row 7: k45, TURN.
Row 9: k1, k2 tog, k38, TURN.
Row 11: k36, TURN.
Continue without further shaping at beginning of row but working 4 sts less on each knit row until down to 8 sts, ending with a purl row.
Change to 2¾mm needles and work in k1 p1 rib for 60 rows. Cast off.

RIGHT LEG

Work as for left leg to ***
Work 52 rows without shaping.
Next row: (with right side facing), k2 tog, knit to end.
Dec in this way on every foll 4th row until 133 sts remain.
Dec for back shaping as for left leg but on purl row, i.e.
Row 1: p1, p2 tog, p56, TURN.
Row 2 and alt rows: Knit.
Complete to match left leg.

GUSSET

With 3¼mm needles cast on 2 sts with MC and working in st st inc 1 st at each end of every alt row until 20 sts are reached, then dec back down to 2 sts.
Cast off.

TO MAKE UP

Refer to 'Tips for the Professional Finish'.

1) Weave in all ends.
2) Block and pin and press, omitting ribbing.
3) Sew leg seams to markers with back stitch.
4) With invisible stitch sew back and front seams to gusset and sew gusset neatly between leg seams.
5) Referring to 'Tips for the Professional Finish' sew elastic in waistband, using second method.

'MITTENS'

KNITTING STANDARD

Description

One-size mitts with inner glove and flip-back top.

Materials

Patons Clansman 4 ply or Beehive 4 ply 3 × 50 gram balls

One set of 4 × 3mm needles.

Measurements

One size (to fit average-size hand)

Tension

28 sts and 36 rows to 10cm sq measured over st st on 3mm needles.

RIGHT HAND

Using 4 double-pointed 3mm needles cast on 48 sts (16 on each of 3 needles), and work in k2 p2 rib for 9cm.
Place a coloured thread on the last stitch to mark the end of rounds.
Next round: Purl 48.

Inner Glove

1st round: Knit.
2nd round: Purl.
Repeat these 2 rounds 9 times, then 1st round once more **

Next round: P2, cast off 11 sts purlwise, p35.
Next round: K2, cast on 7 sts, inc into every
            foll 8th st 4 times (48 sts).
Work 26 rounds g st, finishing on a knit round.
Cast off purlwise.

Outer Glove

Commencing at coloured marker pick up 48 sts through the sts of first purl round.

Next round: * k3, inc into next st, rep from *
            12 times (60 sts). Work in st st for
            9cm ***
Next round: P30, k30.
Next round: K60.
Repeat these 2 rounds once.
Next round: (opening) P2, cast off 26
            purlwise, p2, k30.
Next round: K2, cast on 26, knit to end of
            round.
Next round: P30, k30.
Next round: K60.
Rep these 2 rounds once, then first round once again.
Knit for 12 rounds.

Shape top

1st round: K2, sl 1, k1, psso, k22, k2 tog, tbl1,
            k4, sl 1, k1, psso, k22, k2 tog tbl1,
            k2.
2nd round: Knit.
Continue decreasing in this manner on alternate rounds until 36 sts remain then dec on every round until 20 sts remain.
Divide sts onto 2 needles and cast off.

LEFT HAND

Inner Glove

Work as for right hand to **

FULL MITT

FOLD BACK TO REVEAL
FINGERLESS GLOVE

Next round: Purl 35, cast off 11 sts, p2.
Next round: K1, inc into next st, * k8, inc into
next st, rep from * 3 times, cast
on 7 sts, k2.
Complete as for right hand.

Outer Glove

Work as for right hand to ***

Next round: K30, p30.
Next round: Knit.
Repeat these 2 rounds once.

Next round: (opening) k30, p2, cast off 26, p2.
Complete as for right hand.

TO FINISH

Refer to 'Tips for the Professional Finish'.
Weave in all ends.
With invisible seam sew tops of outer gloves.

'KNITTED SHIRT'

KNITTING STANDARD

See 'Blazer' in Spring.

AUTUMN

Description

Man's 'V' neck cardigan in chunky tweed with oversize Argyll motifs using colour block method and Swiss embroidery, with diamond-pattern cuffs using 'stranding or Fair Isle' technique.

Materials

Rowan Spun Tweed

A – Paprika 5(6) × 100gram balls

B – Cranberry 1(1) × 100 gram ball

C – One a.m. 1(1) × 100 gram ball

Rowan DK (lightweight).

D – Purple 6(6) × 25gram balls

E – Gold 5(5) × 25gram balls

One pair each needles sizes 4½mm and 3¾mm and a stitch holder.

3 leather buttons

Measurements

To fit chest
91–96cm   102–107cm

Actual measurements
124cm   129cm

Length from shoulder
71cm   74cm

Sleeve seam
51cm   53cm

Tension

18 sts and 24 rows to 10cm sq measured over st st on 4½mm needles.

NB Pattern uses colour block, stranding or Fair Isle and embroidery techniques.

BACK

Using 3¾mm needles and D cast on 110(114)sts and work in st st for 22 rows (to form facing).
Change to E and work 2 rows in knit (2nd row will form ridge for fold).
Now place diamonds of 3 sts by 3 rows in D and E using 'stranding or Fair Isle' technique as follows:

Row 1:   K4(0) E, * k1 D, k5 E, rep from * to last 4(0) sts, k1 D, k3(0) E.
Row 2:   P 0(1) D, p2(1) E, * p3 D, p3 E, rep from * to last 6(8) sts, p3 D, p3(3) E, p0(2) D.
Row 3:   As row 1.
Work 2 rows in E only.
Row 6:   P0(2) E, * p1 D, p5 E, rep from * to last 2(4) sts, p1 D, p1(3) E.
Complete diamond as before and work 2 rows straight in E.
Rows 11–20: As rows 1–10.

When 4 sets of diamonds have been worked on trim change to 4½mm needles and using colour block method and stocking stitch work Argyll pattern as follows, using A for main colour and B and C for diamonds, alternately.

Row 1:   K28(30) A, 2 C, 50 A, 2 C, 28(30) A.
Row 2:   P27(29) A, 4 C, 48 A, 4 C, 27(29) A.
Continue in this way increasing diamonds in C by 1 st either side until 32 sts are being worked in diamonds. Work 2 rows with 32 sts then decrease diamonds back down to 2 sts (32 rows).
Work 6 rows st st in A only.

Row 39: Place 2 more diamonds as before using B for C.
Continue as before working diamonds in B ending on row 70.
Work 6 rows in A only.
Continue in this way working a further 2 diamonds in C starting on row 77 and in B starting on row 115, with 6 rows in A between as before.
When work measures 41(42)cm from cast-on edge place coloured threads at each end of row to indicate armhole positions.
Continue, working diamonds, until work measures 68(71)cm from cast-on edge.
Shape shoulders by casting off 12(13) sts at beg of next 2(4) rows, then 13(13) sts at beg of next 4(2) rows. Work 1 row and cast off remaining 34(36) sts.

POCKET LININGS (2 alike both sizes)

With 4½mm and A cast on 26 sts and work in st st for 15cm, leaving sts on a spare needle.

RIGHT FRONT

Using 3¾/4mm needles and D cast on 50(52) sts
and work in st st for 22 rows.
Change to E and knit 2 rows.
Now work 4 sets of diamonds as for back
using 'stranding or Fair Isle' technique setting
pattern as follows:

K1(2)C, * k1D, k5C, rep from * to last 1(2) sts,
k1D, k0(1)C.
Complete trim to match back then change to
4½mm needles and work Argyll patt as
follows:

Row 1:   K29(30) A, 2 C, 19(20) A.
Row 2:   P18(19) A, 4 C, 28(29) A.
Work diamond as for back finishing on row 32.

Row 33: K10 A, leave next 26 sts on stitch
         holder, k14(16) sts in A.
Row 34: Purl, placing pocket lining in place of
         sts cast off in previous row.
Row 39: Knit, placing diamond in B as before.
Whilst keeping to diamond pattern as for back
and marking side seam to indicate armhole
position shape 'V' front as follows:
Starting on rows 73(75) dec 1 st at neck edge
on this row and on foll alt rows 6(6) times, dec
1 st at neck edge on foll 4th rows 3 times, on
foll 6th rows twice, and on foll 8th rows 1(2)
times.
Continue straight on remaining 38(39) sts until
front length is same as back and cast off
shoulders as for one side of back.

LEFT FRONT

Work as for right front, reversing all shapings.

SLEEVES (2 alike)

Using 3¾/4mm needles and D cast on 52(54) sts
and work 22 rows in st st.
Change to E and knit for 2 rows.
Now work 4 sets of diamonds as before setting
pattern as follows:
K2(3) C, * k1 D, k5 C, rep from * to last 2(3) sts,
k1 D, k1(2) C.
Complete trims as for back and fronts.
Change to 4½mm needles and st st and set
diamonds as follows:

Row 1: K25(26) A, 2 C, 25(26) A.
Row 2: P24(25) A, 4 C, 24(25) A.

Continue working diamonds as before but
with only 3 straight rows between whilst AT
THE SAME TIME inc 1 st at each end of next
and every foll 4th row until 96(100) sts are
reached.
Continue without further shaping until work
measures 51(53)cm from cast-on edge. Cast
off.

BUTTONBAND

Referring to 'Tips for the Professional Finish', join shoulder seams with invisible seam.
Using 3¾mm needles and E pick up approx 192(198) sts between bottom front and centre back of neck and work 2 rows of st st.
Using 'stranding or Fair Isle' technique place 3 sets of diamonds as on trims over next 14 rows.

Row 17: Purl (to form ridge) in E.
Row 18: Knit in E.
Change to D and stocking stitch for 16 rows to form facing. Cast off.

BUTTONHOLE BAND

Work as for other front but on rows 9 and 10 make three buttonholes by casting off 3 sts each time and casting on over them again in next row.
Place first buttonhole 2.5cm from bottom front then next two at intervals of approx 14–15cm
Work facing with buttonholes to correspond when folded over.

POCKET TOPS

Pick up 26 sts with 3¾mm needles and using E st st for 2 rows, then on third row place a set of diamonds as follows:
K4 E, *k1 D, k5 E, rep from * to last 4 sts, k1 D, k3 E.
Work diamonds as before then 2 rows of E only.
Row 8: Knit (to form ridge) in E.
Row 9: Knit in E.
Change to D and st st for 8 rows. Cast off.

TO MAKE UP

Refer to 'Tips for the Professional Finish'.

1) Weave in all ends, block and pin and steam.
2) Open out work and set sleeves between markers with an invisible seam.
3) Sew up side and sleeve seams with an invisible seam.
4) Catch down pocket linings to inside with slip stitch.
5) Fold over all trims and hem facings to insides on bottom, sleeves, buttonbands and pocket tops, and slip stitch down.
6) Sew on buttons.
7) Refer to chart for 'Argyll Pattern' and with D, used double, work large crossed diamonds, as indicated by using Swiss embroidery technique, referring to 'Tips for the Professional Finish', or chain stitch.

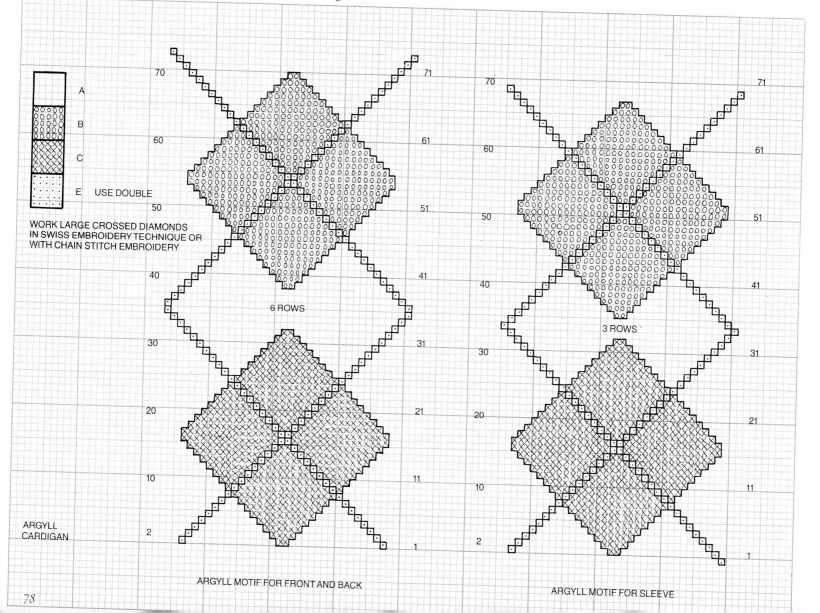

A
B
C
E   USE DOUBLE

WORK LARGE CROSSED DIAMONDS
IN SWISS EMBROIDERY TECHNIQUE OR
WITH CHAIN STITCH EMBROIDERY

6 ROWS

3 ROWS

ARGYLL
CARDIGAN

ARGYLL MOTIF FOR FRONT AND BACK

ARGYLL MOTIF FOR SLEEVE

A U T U M N

Description

Boxy jacket with 'leaf pattern' over dolman-sleeved sweater.

Materials

Scheepjeswol Zermatt 100% pure wool

CARDIGAN

Main col. Green 12(13:14:15:16) × 50 gram balls

1st contrast col. Rust 3(3:3:3:3) × 50 gram balls

2nd contrast. Fashion Lurex 3(3:3:3:3) × 50 gram balls.

SWEATER

Main col. 11(12:13:14:15) × 50 gram balls

1st contrast col. Rust 2(2:2:2:2) × 50 gram balls

2nd contrast col. Gold 2(2:2:2:2) × 50 gram balls.

One pair each needles sizes 4mm and 3¼mm, 3¼mm circular needle.

3 buttons, 2 stitch holders, 1 pair of dolman-shaped shoulder pads for the sweater (optional).

Measurements

To fit bust
81cm–86cm 91cm–96cm 101cm

Actual measurements
95cm–100cm 106cm–111cm 117cm

Length from shoulder
55cm–56cm 57cm–59cm 60cm

Sleeve seam
46cm 47cm 48cm

Tension

22sts and 28 rows to 10cm sq over st st on size 4mm needles.

CARDIGAN
BACK

With 3¼mm needles and MC cast on 105(111:117:123:129) sts.
1st row: K1, p1 to last st, k1.
2nd row: P1, k1 to last st, p1.
These 2 rows form rib.
Rep 1st and 2nd rows 8 more times.

Change to 4mm needles.
Beg with a K row work 2(4:6:8:10) rows in st st.
Cont in st st foll patt set on chart for 64 rows. Mark with a contrast thread.
Cont in patt for 62 rows.

Shape Neck

K33(36:39:42:45), turn, leaving rem sts on a spare needle.
Cont on first sts dec 1 st at the neck edge of the next 9(10:11:12:13) rows.
Work 2(3:4:5:6) rows straight.
Cast off 12(13:14:15:16) sts at the beg of the next row.

P one row. Cast off the rem sts.
Rejoin yarn to sts on spare needle.
K39, put these sts on to a st holder, k33(36:39:42:45).
Work rem sts to match the opposite side.

POCKET BAG (make 2)

With 4mm needles and MC cast on 23 sts.
Work 28 rows in st st, leave sts on a spare needle.

KNITTING STANDARD

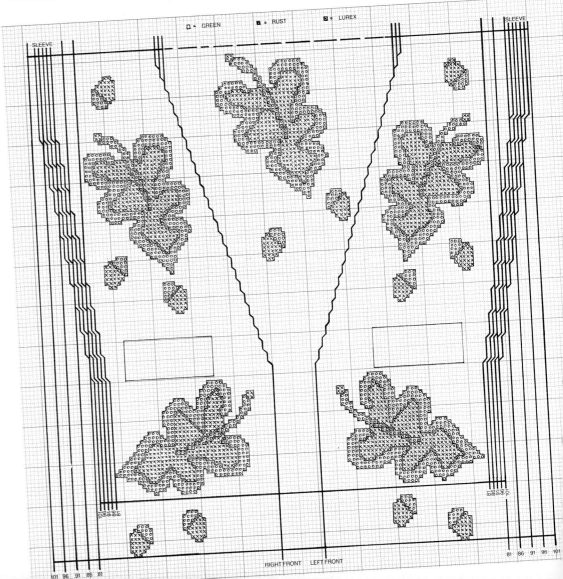

LEFT FRONT

With 3¼mm needles and MC cast on 47(49:53:55:59) sts.
Work 18 rows in rib, inc 1 st at the end of last row on sizes 86 and 96cm [47(50:53:56:59) sts].
Change to 4mm needles.
Beg with a K row work 2(4:6:8:10) rows in st st.
Cont in st st foll patt on chart for 44 rows.

POCKET

K9(12:15:18:21), put the next 23 sts on to a st holder, k23 sts of pocket bag, k15.
P one row.

Shape Neck while cont to foll patt on chart.
Dec 1 st at the neck edge of the next and every foll 3rd row until 24(26:28:30:32) sts rem.
Work straight until the front matches the back at longest point. Cast off.

RIGHT FRONT

Work as left reversing shapings and being sure to place pocket to match left side.

SLEEVES

With 3¼mm needles and MC cast on 65(67:69:71:73) sts.
Work 17 rows in rib.
Inc row: rib 2(3:4:5:6), * inc in next st, rib 1; rep from * ending row rib 2(3:4:5:6) [96(98:100:102:104) sts].
Change to 4mm needles.
Beg with a K row cont in st st, foll patt set on chart for 32 rows.

Shape Sleeve while keeping cont of patt.

Inc 1 st at each end of the next and every foll 6th row until there are 118(120:122:124:126) sts on the needles.
Complete chart.
Work 0(0:2:2:4) rows in st st.
Cast off.

Neck Edge

First join both shoulder seams.
With a 3¼mm circular needle and MC, beg at right front edge pick up and k144(148:152:154:158) sts to shoulder, 10(12:14:15:16) sts down back, k39, pick up and k10(12:14:15:16) sts to shoulder, 144(148:152:154:158) sts to cast-on edge.
Work 7 rows in rib.
Buttonholes: 1st row: rib 5, (cast off 3, rib 24) 3 times, rib to end.
2nd row: work in rib, casting on 3 sts over cast-off sts.
Work 7 more rows in rib. Cast off ribwise.

POCKET WELTS (both alike)

With 4mm needles and MC work 10 rows in rib. Cast off loosely ribwise.

SHOULDER PADS

With 3¼mm needles and MC cast on 39 sts.
Work a square in rib. Cast off ribwise.

TO MAKE UP

All techniques are listed in 'Tips for the Professional Finish'.
1) Weave in ends.
2) Omitting all ribs block out and press.
3) With an invisible seam join sides to contrast thread and sleeve seams.

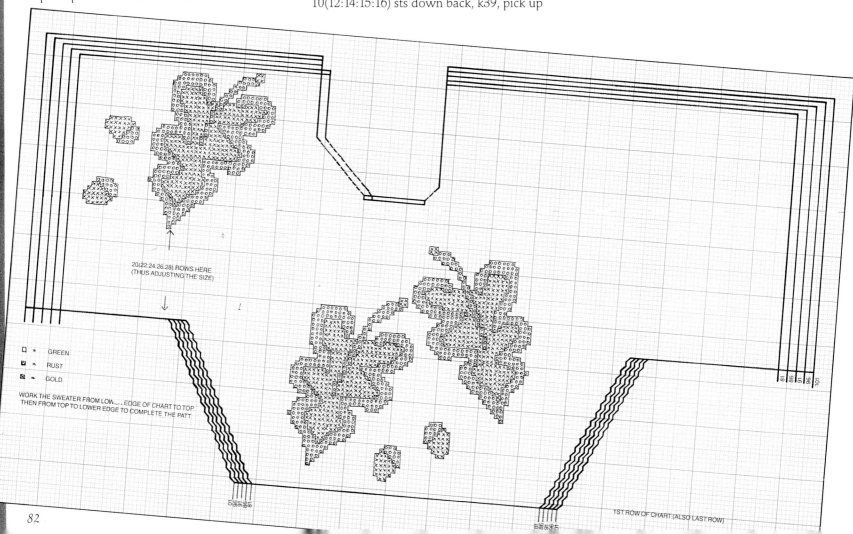

20(22:24:26:28) ROWS HERE
(THUS ADJUSTING THE SIZE)

□ = GREEN

⊡ = RUST

⊠ = GOLD

WORK THE SWEATER FROM LOW... EDGE OF CHART TO TOP,
THEN FROM TOP TO LOWER EDGE TO COMPLETE THE PATT.

1ST ROW OF CHART (ALSO LAST ROW)

4) With an invisible seam sew pocket welts in place.
5) Sew pocket bag in place with a slip stitch.
6) With a back stitch sew in sleeves.
7) Sew in shoulder pads.
8) Sew buttons on to left band.

SWEATER
BODY AND SLEEVES worked in one piece from cuff to cuff.

With 3¼mm needles and MC cast on 45(47:49:51:55) sts.
1st row: K1 p1 to last st, k1.
2nd row: P1 k1 to last st, p1.
These 2 rows form rib, rep 1st and 2nd rows 9 more times.
Change to 4mm needles.
Beg with a K row cont in st st inc 1 st at each end of every 6th row until there are 67(69:71:73:77) sts.
Now beg to foll patt on chart, at the same time inc 1 st at each end of every foll WS row until there are 101(103:105:107:111) sts.
Cast on 29(30:31:32:33) sts at the beg of the next 2 rows [159(163:167:171:177) sts].
Work 26(28:30:32:34) rows.

Shape Neck

K79(81:83:85:88), turn, leaving rem sts on a spare needle.
Cont on first sts dec 1 st at the inner edge of the next 3 rows.
Work 50(52:54:56:58) rows, now inc 1 st at the inner edge of the next 3 rows. Leave sts on needle.
Rejoin yarn to sts on spare needle.
Cast off 12(12:14:14:14), k to end.
Dec 1 st at the inner edge of the next 12 rows.
Work 32(34:36:38:40) rows, now inc 1 st at the inner edge of the next 12 rows.
Next row: P, cast on 12(12:14:14:14), p sts on spare needle [159(163:167:171:177) sts].
Work 26(28:30:32:34) rows.
Cast off 29(30:31:32:33) sts at the beg of the next 2 rows [101(103:105:107:111) sts].
Dec 1 st at each end of next and every foll alt row until 67(69:71:73:77) sts rem.
Dec 1 st at each end of 2nd and every foll 6th row until 45(47:49:51:55) sts rem. Work 5 rows.
Change to 3¼mm needles.
Work 20 rows in rib. Cast off loosely ribwise.

MAIN BODY (back and front alike)

With 4mm needles and MC, with right side facing pick up and k93(99:105:111:117) sts evenly along edge.
Work 7(8:9:9:10) cm in rib.
Change to 3¼mm needles.

DIAG. AUTUMN LEAVES SWEATER.
CUFF
18.5(19:20:21:22)
46
CUFF
36.5(37.5:38.5:39.5:40.5)
40.5(43:45:47:49)
31(32:33:34:35)

Cont in rib until 18(19:20:21:22)cm have been worked.
Change to 4mm needles.
Cont in rib until 31(32:33:34:35)cm have been worked.
Cast off loosely ribwise.

COLLAR

With a 3¼mm circular needle, MC and RS facing, pick up and k134(138:142:146:150) sts evenly round neck edge.

Cont in rounds working k1 p1 rib until the collar measures 10cm.
Change to a 4mm needle.
Cont in rib until the collar measures 21cm.
Cast off loosely ribwise.

TO MAKE UP

1) Weave in all ends.
2) With an invisible seam join both side/underarm seams.
3) Sew in shoulder pads.

AUTUMN

Description

Big drop-sleeve sweater in reverse stocking stitch with wide double cable at centre of front, back and sleeves.

Materials

Rowan Cotton Chenille 7(7:8) × 100 gram hanks

One pair each needles sizes 4½mm and 3¾mm

Measurements

To fit chest
91–96cm   96–102cm   102–107cm

Actual measurements
117cm   122cm   127cm

Length from shoulder
73cm   76cm   79cm

Sleeve seam
46cm   48cm   51cm

Tension

16 sts and 34 rows to 10cm sq measured over rev st st on 4½mm needles.

Abbreviations used in cable panel

C5L (cross 5 left): slip next 4 sts onto a cable needle and hold at front of work, purl next st on left-hand needle, then knit sts from cable needle.

C5R (cross 5 right): slip the next st onto a cable needle and hold at back of work, knit next 4 sts from the left-hand needle, then purl the st from the cable needle.

C8B: slip the next 4 sts onto a cable needle and hold at back of work, knit the next 4 sts from the left-hand needle then knit the 4 sts from cable needle.

Instructions for cable panel worked over 28 sts and 30 rows

Row 1: K4, p6, k8, p6, k4
Row 2: P4, k6, p8, k6, p4
Row 3: K4, p6, C8B, p6, k4
Row 4: As row 2
Row 5: C5L, p4, C5R, C5L, p4, C5R
Row 6: K1, p4, k4, p4, k2, p4, k4, p4, k1
Row 7: P1, C5L, p2, C5R, p2, C5L, p2, C5R, p1
Row 8: K2, p4, k2, p4, k4, p4, k2, p4, k2
Row 9: P2, C5L, C5R, p4, C5L, C5R, p2
Row 10: K3, p8, k6, p8, k3

Row 11: P3, C8B, p6, C8B, p3
Row 12: As row 10
Row 13: P3, k8, p6, k8, p3
Row 14: As row 10
Row 15: As row 13
Row 16: As row 10
Row 17: As row 11
Row 18: As row 10
Row 19: P2, C5R, C5L, p4, C5R, C5L, p2
Row 20: As row 8
Row 21: P1, C5R, p2, C5L, p2, C5R, p2, C5L, p1
Row 22: As row 6
Row 23: C5R, p4, C5L, C5R, p4, C5L
Row 24: As row 2
Row 25: As row 3
Row 26: As row 2
Row 27: As row 1
Row 28: As row 2
Row 29: As row 1
Row 30: As row 2

Repeat these 30 rows throughout for cable panel which will be referred to as patt 28.

BACK

With 3¾mm needles cast on 92(96:100) sts and work in k2 p2 rib for 9cm, increasing 4 sts evenly over last row [96(100:104)].
Change to 4½mm needles and set pattern as follows:

Row 1: Purl 34(36:38), patt 28, row 1, p34(36:38).

Row 2: Knit 34(36:38), patt 28, row 2, k34(36:38).

Continue straight working rev st st sides and following instructions for cable panel until work measures 44(46:47)cm from cast-on edge.
Mark each end of next row with a coloured thread to indicate armhole position.
Continue until work measures 71(74:76)cm from cast-on edge.

Shape shoulders by casting off as follows:

11(11:12) sts at beg of next 2 rows,
11(12:12) sts at beg of next 2 rows,

12(12:12) sts at beg of next 2 rows.
Cast off remaining 28(30:32) sts.

FRONT

Work as for back until work measures 63(66:68)cm from cast-on edge.
Divide for neck shaping as follows:
Next row: Cast off centre 6(8:10) sts.
Work on each set of sts separately as follows:
Dec 1 st at neck edge on following 6 rows, then dec 1 st at neck edge on the following alternate row 5 times.
Continue straight until front matches back to shoulder shaping and cast off at shoulders to match back.

SLEEVES

With 3¾mm needles cast on 44(44:48) sts and work in k2 p2 rib for 9cm, increasing 4(6:4) sts evenly over last row [48(50:52) sts].
Change to 4mm and set pattern as follows:
Row 1: P10(11:12), patt 28, row 1, p10(11:12).
Row 2: K10(11:12), patt 28, row 2, k10(11:12).
Continue in rev st st with centre cable panel, AT THE SAME TIME inc 1 st at each end of every 4th row until 88(92:96) sts are reached.
Continue straight until work measures 46(48:51)cm from cast-on edge. Cast off.
Work another sleeve alike.

COLLAR

With 3½mm needles cast on 84(88:92) sts and work in k2 p2 rib for 9 cm.
Cast off firmly in rib.

TO MAKE UP

Refer to 'Tips for the Professional Finish'.

1) Weave in all ends
2) Block and pin and steam, omitting all ribbing.
3) Lay work out flat and join shoulders with an invisible seam.
4) Place sleeve tops between markers and sew with an invisible seam.
5) With an invisible seam sew sleeve seams and side seams.
   Sew on collar (placing join at shoulder edge).
6) Slip stitch into position.

AUTUMN

Description

Raglan-sleeve cardigan in 1950s American style with colour-block country scene motifs, with garter stitch button front, collar and pocket details.

Materials

Forsells Slalom Aran Pure New Wool

A – Ember Red 14(14:15) × 50 gram balls

B – Spice 1(1:1:1) × 50 gram ball

C – Gorse 1(1:1:1) × 50 gram ball

D – Scoured White 1(1:1:1) × 50 gram ball

E – Heather 1(1:1:1) × 50 gram ball

F – Teal 1(1:1:1) × 50 gram ball

G – Black 1(1:1:1) × 50 gram ball

Forsell Anglia Tweed Aran Pure New Wool (or similar)

H – Cleveland Brown 3(3:3) × 50 gram balls

One pair each needles sizes 4mm and 5mm and spare needles

6 leather buttons

Measurements

To fit chest
86–91cm   97–102cm   107–112cm

Actual measurements
117cm   122cm   127cm

Length from shoulder
74cm   76cm   79cm

Sleeve seam
43cm   44cm   46cm

Tension

18 sts and 24 rows to 10cm sq measured over st st on 5mm needles.

NB Pattern uses colour block method.

BACK

With 4mm needles and A cast on 96(100:104) sts and work in k1 p1 rib for 8cm.

Inc row: Rib 8(10:12), * inc into next st, rib 10, rep from * 7 times, inc into next st, rib to end [104(108:112)].
Change to 5mm needles and st st and work 5 rows (end WS facing).
Place motif 1 on 6th row 33(35:37) sts in from side.

Work motif from chart, using colour block method.

At the same time when work measures 46(47:47)cm from cast-on edge shape raglan as follows:
Cast off 3(4:4) sts at beg of next 2 rows, then dec 1 st at each end of next 2(2:2) rows.
Now dec 1 st at each end of every alt row until 28(30:30) sts remain.
Cast off.

POCKET LININGS (2 alike)

With A and 5mm needles cast on 23(25:25) sts and work in st st for 13(14:15)cm leaving sts on a spare needle.

RIGHT FRONT

With 4mm needles and A cast on 46(49:52) sts and work in k1 p1 rib for 8cm.

Inc row: Rib 9, * inc into next st, rib 8(9:10) 3 times, inc into next st, rib to end [50(53:56) sts].
Change to 5mm needles and work in st st until work measures 18.5(20:20.5)cm from cast-on edge.

Place pocket top as follows:

With right side facing, k11(10:11), k23(25:25) sts for pocket, k16(18:20).

Next row: P16(18:20), k23(25:25), p11(10:11). Repeat these 2 rows until garter stitch pocket top measures 2.5cm.

Next row: K11(10:11), cast off 23(25:25), k16(18:20).

Next row: Purl, working pocket lining in place of stitches cast off in previous row.

Place motif 2 as follows on row 35 (count st st rows only).

Row 35: K14 A, k3 from motif, k to end in A.
Continue in st st working motif from chart.

Row 59: (Place motif 3) k21 A, k6 from motif, k to end in A.
Continue in st st working motif from chart.
When work measures 46(47:47)cm from cast-on edge shape raglan as follows:
With wrong side facing cast off 3(4:4) sts at beg of next row, then dec 1 st at raglan edge on next 2 rows, then dec 1 st on alt rows until 21(22:22) sts remain.

Shape neck

Whilst keeping continuity of raglan shaping cast off 5(5:5) sts at neck edge on next row, then dec 1 st at neck edge on the next 5 rows, then dec 1 at neck edge on alt rows until 1 st remains. Cast off.

LEFT FRONT

Work as for right front reversing all shapings and placing motif for left front as follows:

Row 49: K27(29:31) A, k8 from motif, k to end in A.
Complete the motif 4 for left front whilst working this side to match right.

LEFT SLEEVE

With 4mm needles and A cast on 52(56:60) sts and work in k1 p1 rib for 8cm.

Inc row: Rib 9(10:10), * inc into next st, rib 10(11:12), rep from * 3 times, inc into next st, rib to end [56(60:64) sts].
Change to 5mm needles and st st increasing 1 st at each end of every foll 5th row until 86(90:94) sts are reached.
Place pheasant motif 5 as follows:

Row 25: K14(16:18) A, k3 from motif, k to end in A.
Work motif from chart whilst completing sleeve increases.
Continue on 86(90:94) sts until work measures 43(44:46)cm from cast-on edge.

Shape raglan as follows:

Cast off 3(4:4) sts at beg of next 2 rows, then dec 1 st at each end of next 2 rows, then dec 1 st at each end of every alt row until 18(20:22) sts remain ***
Keeping continuity of decreases on right-hand side as before shape top as follows:
With wrong side facing, cast off 4(4:4) sts at beg of next 2 alt rows, then cast off 3(4:5) sts at beg of next 2 alt rows. Cast off.

RIGHT SLEEVE

Work as for left sleeve to ***
Reverse the top shaping with right side facing and keeping alt row shaping on left side of work.

BUTTON BAND

With 4mm needles and A cast on 7 sts and work in g st until work is long enough (when slightly stretched) to go up left front. Cast off.

BUTTONHOLE BAND

Working as for other band make 6 buttonholes by casting off centre 3 sts and casting on 3 sts over them in next row.

Place first buttonhole 2.5cm from bottom, with 5 more at intervals of approx 12(13:14)cm with last buttonhole 2.5cm from top.

COLLAR

With 4mm needles and A cast on 7 sts and work in g st.

Row 1:   Knit.
Row 2:   K2, inc into next st, k to last 3 sts, inc into next st, k2.
Repeat these 2 rows until 17 sts are reached.

Row 9:   Knit.
Row 10:   K2, inc into next st, knit to end.
Repeat these 2 rows until 23 sts are reached and work straight for 36cm.
Now decrease back down as follows:

Row 1:   Knit to last 4 sts, k2 tog, k2.
Row 2:   Knit.
Repeat these 2 rows until 17 sts remain.

Row 15:   K2, k2 tog, k to last 4 sts, k2 tog, k2.
Row 16:   Knit.
Repeat these 2 rows until 7 sts remain. Cast off.

TO MAKE UP

Refer to 'Tips for the Professional Finish'.

1) Weave in all ends.
2) Block and pin and steam.
3) With invisible seam, sew raglan seams.
4) Sew sleeve seam and side seams with invisible seam.
5) Slip stitch pocket linings into position on inside.
6) Sew on button and buttonhole bands.
7) Fold collar in half, pin centre, open out, and placing centre of collar to centre of back of neck sew on collar, easing collar towards front on either side (straight edge of collar to finish just behind button and buttonhole bands).
8) Sew on buttons.

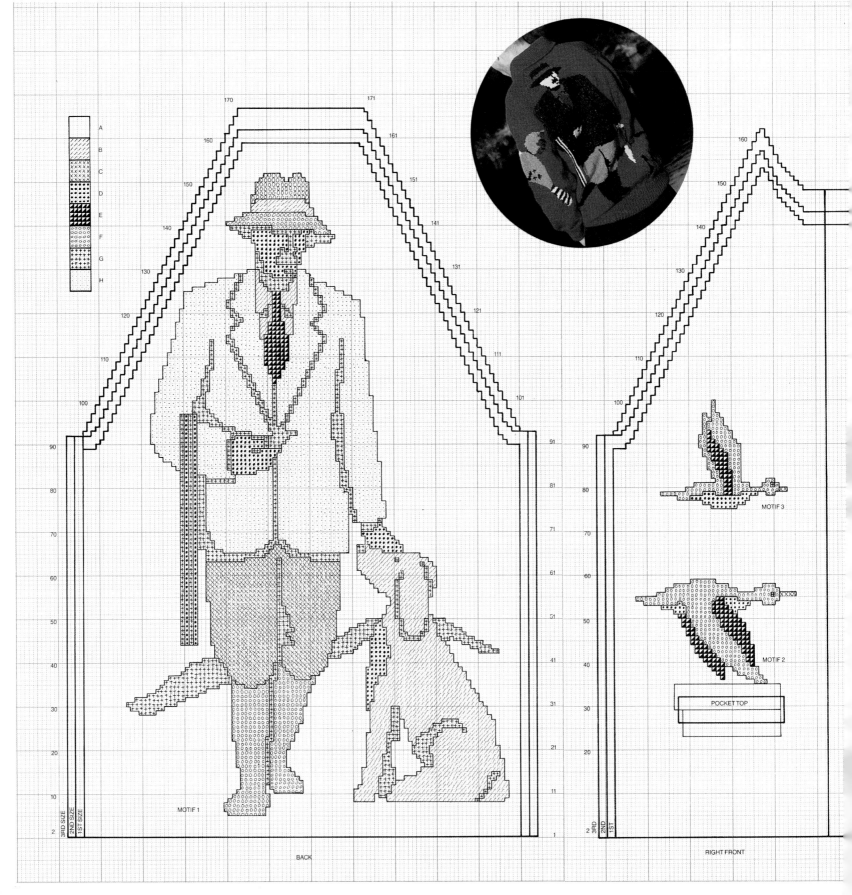

88

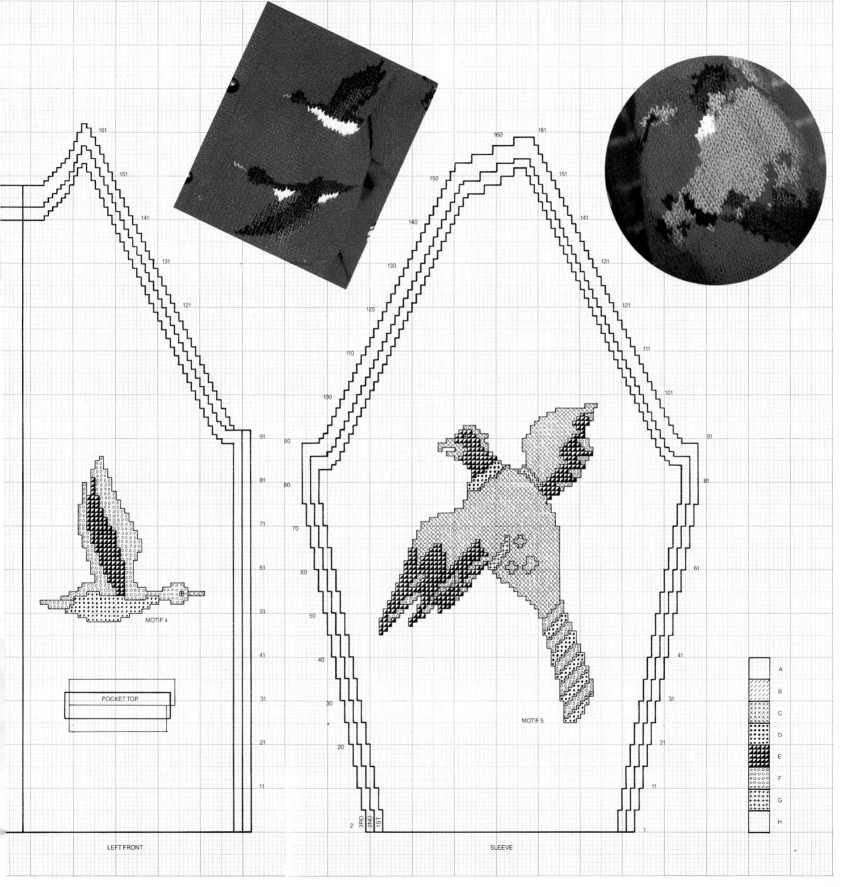

161

151

141

131

121

91

81

71

61

51

MOTIF 4

POCKET TOP

41

31

21

11

LEFT FRONT

160   161

150   151

140   141

130   131

120   121

110   111

100   101

90   91

80   81

70   81

60   61

50   41

40   31

30   21

20   11

2
3RD
2ND
1ST   1

MOTIF 5

SLEEVE

A
B
C
D
E
F
G
H

AUTUMN

Description

Top and skirt in moss stitch with collar, cuffs, waist and hem worked in Fair Isle pattern.

Materials

Schachenmayr Extra DK.

Sweater

MC – Gold 10(11:12:13) × 50 gram balls

C – Brown 2(2:2:2) × 50 gram balls

Skirt

MC – Gold 5(5:6:7) × 50 gram balls

C – Brown 2(2:2:2) × 50 gram balls

One pair each needles sizes 4mm and 3¼mm, 1 circular needle size 4mm.

Elastic 2.5 cm wide to fit waist.

Sweater Measurements

To fit bust
81cm–86cm 91cm–96cm

Actual measurements

90cm	95cm	102cm	108cm

Length from shoulder

53cm	54cm	55cm	56cm

Sleeve seam

43cm	43cm	43cm	43cm

Skirt Measurements

To fit hips

86cm	91cm	96cm	101cm

Actual measurements

91cm	97cm	102cm	108cm

Length from waist

46cm	47cm	48cm	49cm

Additional Abbreviation: m st = moss stitch.

Tension

22 sts and 28 rows to 10 cm sq measured over m st on size 4mm needles.

BACK

With 4mm needles and MC cast on 89(95:101:107) sts.

1st row: K1, p1 to last st, k1

2nd row: P1, k1 to last st, p1.

KNITTING STANDARD ✗✗✗

These 2 rows form the rib, rep 1st and 2nd rows 3 more times.

Cont in st st foll patt set on chart for 34 rows.

Cont in m st as follows:

K1, p1 to last st, k1. This row makes m st.

Cont in m st inc 1 st at each end of every 6th row until there are 99(105:113:119) sts on the needles.

Cont in m st until the back measures 29(30:31:32)cm from cast-on edge, ending with a WS row.

Shape Armholes while keeping cont of m st.

Cast off 3 sts at the beg of the next 4 rows.

Dec 1 st at each end of the next 4(6:8:10) rows, work one row.

Dec on the next and 2 foll alt rows [73(75:79:81) sts]. **

Cont in m st until the back measures 24cm from the beg of armhole shaping ending with a WS row.

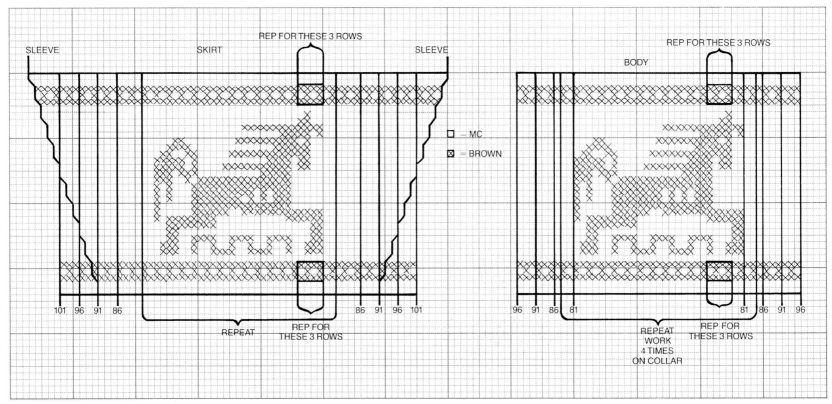

SLEEVE   SKIRT   REP FOR THESE 3 ROWS   SLEEVE

□ = MC
☒ = BROWN

101 96 91 86   86 91 96 101

REPEAT   REP FOR THESE 3 ROWS

REP FOR THESE 3 ROWS   BODY

96 91 86 81   81 86 91 96

REPEAT WORK 4 TIMES ON COLLAR   REP FOR THESE 3 ROWS

Cast off 13(14:16:17), patt 47, cast off the rem 13(14:16:17) sts.
Leave the rem sts on a spare needle.

FRONT

Work as back to **
Cont in m st until the front measures 14cm from the beg of the armhole shaping ending with a WS row.

Shape Neck while keeping the cont of m st:
m st 23(24.25.26), turn, leaving the rem sts on a spare needle.
Cont on first sts dec 1 st at the neck edge of every row until 13(14:16:17) sts rem.
Work straight until the front matches the back. Cast off.
Rejoin the yarn to sts on spare needle.
Patt 27, put these sts on a st holder, m st to end.
Work the rem 23(24:26:27) sts to match the opposite side.

SLEEVES (both alike, all sizes)

With 3¼mm needles and MC cast on 45 sts.
Work 8 rows in rib.
Change to 4mm needles.
Cont in st st foll patt set on chart for 34 rows, AT THE SAME TIME shape the sleeve by inc 1 st at each end of every 3rd row.
Cont in m st still inc on every 3rd row until there are 111 sts on the needles.
Cont in m st until the sleeve measures 43cm

from cast-on edge, ending with a WS row.

Shape Top while keeping cont of patt.
Cast off 3 sts at the beg of the next 4 rows.
Dec 1 st at each end of the next and every foll alt row until 75 sts rem.
Cast off 3 sts at the beg of the next 6 rows. Cast off the rem sts.

COLLAR

First join both shoulder seams.

With a 4mm circular needle and MC pick up and k 25 sts from left shoulder down front neck edge to sts on st holder, k27, pick up and k25 sts to right shoulder seam, k47 sts of back neck [124 sts].
Work 34 rounds in st st foll patt set on chart.
P next row to mark fold.
Work 34 more rounds in st st (with MC only).
Cast off.

SHOULDER PADS make 2

With 3¼mm needles and MC cast on 39 sts.
Work a square in rib. Cast off ribwise.

TO MAKE UP

All the techniques are listed in 'Tips for the Professional Finish'.
1) Weave in all ends.
2) With a slip stitch sew collar in place.
3) With an invisible seam join sides and sleeves.

4) Sew sleeves into the armhole using a back stitch and gauging the top to fit the armhole.
5) Sew in shoulder pads.

SKIRT (Make 2 pieces)

With 3¼mm needles and MC cast on 101(107:113:119) sts.
Work 8 rows in rib.
Change to 4mm needles.
Cont in st st foll patt set on chart for 34 rows.
Cont in m st until the skirt measures 36(37:38:39)cm from cast-on edge, ending with a WS row.
Change to 3¼mm needles.
Cont in m st dec 1 st at each end of the next and every foll 6th row until 89(95:101:107) sts rem.
Work the WS row.
Beg with a K row work 9 rows in st st.
K one row to mark fold, work 8 more rows in st st.
Cast off.

TO MAKE UP

All techniques are listed in 'Tips for the Professional Finish'.
1) Weave in all ends.
2) With an invisible seam join sides.
3) Fold hem over the elastic.

AUTUMN

Description

Three-piece suit, top with shaped and thonged edges and cables over dolman-sleeved sweater and flared skirt.

Materials

Hayfield Lugano

Top: 7(8) × 50 gram balls

Skirt: 9(11) × 50 gram balls

Sweater:

Hayfield Grampion DK

8(9:10:11:12) × 50 gram balls

One pair each needles sizes 5½mm and 4½mm for Top and Skirt.

1 cable needle.

10 metres leather thonging for Top

Elastic 2.5cm wide to fit waist for the Skirt.

Measurements

To fit bust
81–86cm   91–96cm

Actual measurements
101cm   112cm

Length from shoulder to shortest point
32cm   33cm

Sleeve seam
46cm   47cm

Additional Abbreviations

CR8 = cross 8, sl the next 4 sts onto a cable needle, hold at the front of work, k4, k sts on the cable needle; TW2 = twist 2, k2 tog, do not drop sts from needle, k first st again, drop sts from needles.

Tension

16 sts and 10 rows to 10cm sq measured over st st on size 5½mm needles.

TOP
BACK

With 5½mm needles cast on 10 sts.

1st row: (right side) k.

2nd row: k1, m1, p8, m1, k1.

3rd row: k1, p1, CR8, p1, k1.

4th row: k1, m1, k1, p8, k1, m1, k1.

5th row: k1, p2, k8, p2, k1.

6th row: k1, m1, k2, p8, k2, m1, k1.

7th row: k1, p3, k8, p3, k1.

8th row: k1, m1, k3, p8, k3, m1, k1.

These 8 rows set patt.

Cont as set m1 st at each end of every WS row until there are 28(30) sts on the needle, ending with a RS row.

Leave sts on needle, break off yarn.

Rep from beg twice more leaving yarn attached to last sts [84(90) sts].

Next row: Cast on 2, * k10(11), p8, k10(11), cast on 2; rep from * to end. Mark with contrast thread [92(98) sts].

Next row: k2, * p10(11), k8, p10(11), TW2; rep from * once more, p10(11), k8, p10(11), k2.

Next row: k1, p1, * k10(11), p8, k10(11), p2; rep from * once more, k10(11), p8, k10(11), p1, k1.

The last 2 rows set patt.

Cont in patt working the cable on appropriate row until back measures 10(11)cm from thread, ending with a WS row.

Shape Armholes while keeping cont of patt.

Cast off 3 sts at beg of next 4 rows.

Dec 1 st at each end of next 2(3) rows [76 (80) sts]. **

Cont on the rem sts until back measures 22cm,

from beg of armhole shaping, ending with a WS row.

Shape Neck while keeping cont of patt.

Patt 22(23), turn, leaving rem sts on a spare needle.

Cont on first sts, dec 1 st at the neck edge of the foll 3 rows.

Work 4 rows. Cast off.

Rejoin yarn to sts on spare needle.

Patt 32(34), put these sts on st holder, patt to end.

Work rem sts to match opposite side.

FRONT

Work as Back to **

Cont on rem sts until front measures 12cm from beg of armhole shaping, ending with a WS row.

Shape Neck while keeping cont of patt.

Patt 37(39), turn, leaving rem sts on a spare needle.

Cont on first sts dec 1 st at the neck edge of every row until 19(20) sts rem.

Work straight until Front matches Back. Cast off.

Rejoin yarn to sts on spare needle.

K2 tog, put this st on a safety pin, patt to end.

Work rem sts to match opposite side.

SLEEVES (both alike)

With 4½mm needles cast on 39 sts.

1st row: k1, p1 to last st, k1.

2nd row: p1, k1 to last st, p1.

These 2 rows form rib.

Cont in rib until cuff measures 18cm.

Inc 1 st at each end of next and every foll 4th row until there are 45 sts on needle, while keeping cont of rib.

Cont in rib until the cuff measures 24cm, ending with 1st row.

Inc row: Rib 2, inc in foll 41 sts, rib 2 [86 sts].

Change to 5½mm needles.

1st row (right side), k1, p25, TW2, p11, k8, p11, TW2, p25, k1.

2nd row: k26, p2, k11, p8, k11, p2, k26.

3rd row: k1, p25, TW2, p11, CR8, p11, TW2, p25, k1.

4th row: as 2nd.
5th to 8th rows: as 1st and 2nd.

These 8 rows form patt.

Cont in patt until sleeve measures 22(23)cm from last row of rib, ending with same row of patt as at beg of armhole shaping.

Shape Sleeve while keeping cont of patt.
Cast off 3 sts at the beg of next 4 rows.
Dec 1 st at each end of next 3 rows, work 1 row.
Dec 1 st at each end of next and every foll alt row until 44 sts rem.
Cast off 3 sts at the beg of next 4 rows.
Cast off rem 32 sts in k2 tog [16 sts]. Cast off.

NECK EDGE

First join right shoulder seam.

With 5½mm needles pick up and k24 sts evenly down left front neck, k st on safety pin at centre front, pick up and k24 sts to shoulder seam, 5 sts to sts on st holder, k10(11), (k2 tog, k3) twice, k2 tog, k10(11), pick up and k 5 sts [88(90) sts].

Work 6 rows in rib dec 1 st at either side of centre front st on every alt row.

Cast off in rib dec on this row also.

SHOULDER PADS

With 5½mm needles cast on 1/ sts.

Work a square in st st. Cast off.

TO MAKE UP

Check techniques with 'Tips for the Professional Finish'.

1) Weave in all ends.
2) Join left shoulder and neckband with invisible seam.
3) With an invisible seam join side and sleeve seams.
4) With a back stitch set in sleeves, gathering the top to fit armhole.
5) Sew shoulder pads in place.
6) Bind the hem and cuffs with thonging.

SKIRT

With 5½mm needles cast on 210(220) sts.

K2 rows. Cont as follows:

1st row: (right side) k1, p16(17), * k8, p16(17), TW2, p16(17); rep from * to last 25(26) sts, k8, p16(17), k1.

2nd row: k17(18), * p8, k16(17), p2, k16(17); rep from * to last 25(26) sts, p8, k17(18).

3rd row: k1, p16(17), * CR8, p16(17), TW2, p16(17); rep from * to last 25(26) sts, CR8, p16(17), k1.

4th row: as 2nd.

5th to 8th rows: as 1st and 2nd.

These 8 rows set patt rep 1st row.

Shape Skirt

10th row: k1, dec 1, k14(15), * p8, k14(15), dec 1, p2, dec 1, k14(15); rep from * to last 25 (26) sts, p8, k14(15), dec 1, k1.

11th to 16th rows: as 3rd to 8th allowing for dec sts.

17th row: as 1st allowing for dec sts.

18th row: k1, dec 1, k13(14), * p8, k13(14), dec 1, p2, dec 1, k13(14): rep from * to last 24(25) sts, p8, k13(14), dec 1, k1.

19th to 24th rows: as 11th to 17th rows.

Cont in this way dec on next and every 8th row until there are 80(90) sts left on needle.

Work 2 rows in patt dec 1 st at end of last row [79(89) sts].

Change to 4½mm needles.

Cont in rib dec 1 st at each end of every 3rd row until 53(57) sts rem. Work 8 rows. Cast off in rib.

TO MAKE UP

Check techniques with 'Tips for the Professional Finish'.

1) Weave in all ends.
2) With an invisible seam join sides.
3) Make herringbone casing for the elastic.

SWEATER

Work as patt for Autumn Leaves, omitting patt on chart and collar and making the cuffs 24 rows in rib longer [44 rows in rib].

COLLAR

With a contrast thread mark centre back and front neck.
With a 3¼mm circular needle pick up and k66(68:70:72:74) sts from contrast thread at centre front along right neck edge to centre back and 66(68:70:72:74) sts round left neck edge to centre front.
Cont in rounds work 7cm in k1 p1 rib.
Next round: M1, rib to end.
Cont in rounds, keeping cont of rib and inc 1 st either side of centre front st (made st) on every row for 38 rows.
Cast off loosely.

MAKE UP as for Autumn Leaves.

With leather thonging bind collar edge. Make a tassel with the remaining leather, fasten to point of collar.

AUTUMN

Description

Large, drop-shoulder sweater worked in tweed, with contrast melange ribs and oversize shawl-collar details.

Materials

Patons

MC – *Chunky Twirl* 10 × 50 gram balls

C – *Clansman DK* 5 × 50 gram balls

– *Diploma 4 ply* 5 × 50 gram balls

NB Clansman and Diploma are used together as 1 yarn and are described as C.

One pair each needles sizes 6mm and 5mm

Measurements

To fit chest
91–102cm   102–112cm

Actual measurements
117cm   127cm

Length from shoulder
70cm   74cm

Sleeve seam
48cm   51cm

Tension

15sts and 20 rows to 10cm sq measured over st st on 6mm needles.

BACK

With 5mm needles and C cast on 78(80) sts and work in k1 p1 rib for 9cm.
Inc row: Rib 7(4), * inc into next st, rib 8(7), to last 8(4) sts, inc into next st, rib to end [86(90) sts]. ***
Change to 6mm needles and MC and work in st st until work measures 41(43)cm from cast-on edge.
Place a coloured thread at each end of next row to indicate armholes.
Continue in st st until work measures 69(71)cm.

Shape shoulders by casting off 5(5) sts at beg of next 2 rows, then 5(6) sts at beg of next 4 rows. Work 1 row.
Cast off remaining 56 sts.

FRONT

Work as for Back to ***
Change to 6mm needles and MC and work in st st until work measures 26(28)cm from cast-on edge, ending RS facing.
Next row: K15(17), cast off next 56 sts, k15(17), and work on each set of sts in turn.

Right Front

Cont straight until work measures 41(43)cm from cast-on edge and place a coloured thread at side edge to indicate armhole position.
Cont straight until work measures 69(71)cm, end WS facing.

Shape shoulder by casting off 5(5) sts at beg of next row, then 5(6) sts at beg of next 2 alt rows.
Rejoin yarn to left front and work to match right, reversing all shapings.

SLEEVES (2 alike)

With 5mm needles and C cast on 41(45) sts and work in k1 p1 rib for 9cm.
Inc row: Rib 5(7), * inc into next st, rib 9, rep from * to last 6(8) sts, inc into next st, rib to end [45(49) sts].
Change to 6mm needles and MC and work in st st, AT THE SAME TIME inc 1 st at each end of every 4th row until 79(83) sts are reached.
Continue without further shaping until work measures 48(51)cm.
Cast off evenly.

COLLAR (Shawl)

With 5mm needles and C cast on 56 sts and work in st st as follows:
Row 1: K56 sts.
Row 2: K3, p53 sts.
Repeat these 2 rows until work measures 132(137)cm.
Cast off.

TO MAKE UP

Refer to 'Tips for the Professional Finish'.

1) Weave in all ends. Graft shoulder seams.
2) Block and pin.
3) Press, omitting all the ribbing.
4) Set in sleeves between armhole markers, making sure that sleeve lies flat, and sew, using invisible seam.
5) Sew side and sleeve seams, with an invisible seam.
6) Set in collar.
   Pin centre of collar, fold in half and pin to centre back of sweater with garter stitch border to outside.
   Pin bottom corners of collar to bottom opening, sew into position using an invisible seam.
   LEFT over RIGHT for men and RIGHT over LEFT for women. Slip stitch underside of collar at back of work.

**"Jack Frost dancing
bespangled in the sunshine"**

Winston Churchill

W I N T E R

Instead of studs try coloured stones diamantés or pearls

Buttons are the finishing touch!

Hunt out old and ornate ones to create interest!

T H E   P A T T E R N S

KNITTING STANDARD ✕✕

Description

Big raglan-sleeve sweater worked in big texture and cable pattern with cable collar detail.

Materials

'MANS OATES'
MC – *Twilleys Dishcloth Cotton* 12(12:13) × 100 gram balls
C – *Twilleys Lyscordet Black*

1 pair each needles size 6½mm and 5mm and a cable needle and stitch holder.

'WOMANS OATES'
MC – *Wendy Sarto* – Cream 10(11:11) × 50gram balls
C – *Wendy Donna* – Grey 6(6:6) × 50gram balls

1 pair each needles sizes 7mm and 6mm and a cable needle and stitch holder.

Measurements

To fit chest/bust size
81–86cm   91–96cm   101–106cm

Actual size
122cm   127cm   132cm

Length from shoulder
65cm   69cm   73cm

Sleeve seam
46cm   48cm   50cm

Tension

10 sts and 16 rows to 10cm sq measured over moss st patt on 6½mm needles.

Moss stitch pattern (worked on an even number of sts)

lst row: (RS facing) *k1, p1,* rep from * to * to end.

2nd row: *p1, k1,* rep from * to * to end.

These 2 rows form the moss stitch pattern and are repeated as required.

NB This pattern uses colour block method.

BACK

With 5mm needles and C cast on 56(60:64) sts. Work in k1 p1 rib for 8cm, on last row of rib inc 9 sts evenly, across row [65(69:73) sts]. Change to 6½mm needles and using MC over moss st and C over cable pattern, work as follows:

1st row: (RS facing) work 28(30:32) sts in MC in moss st, leave yarn hanging and introduce C, twisting yarns at back of work to avoid a hole, K9 in C, introduce another ball MC and work 28(30:32) sts in moss st.

2nd row: Work 28(30:32) sts in MC in moss st, p9 sts in C, moss st 28(30:32) in MC.

Repeat last 2 rows once more.

5th row: Work 28(30:32) sts in MC in moss st, slip next 3 sts onto cable needle and leave at back of work, with C k next 3 sts, then k3 sts from cable needle, k3 in C.

Work 28(30:32) sts in moss st in MC

6th row: As 2nd row.

7th–10th rows: As 1st–4th rows.

11th row: Work 28(30:32) sts in MC in moss st, with C k next 3 sts, slip next 3 sts onto cable needle and leave at front of work, k3 sts in C, then k the 3 sts from cable needle, work 28(30:32) sts in moss st in MC.

12th row: As 2nd row.

These 12 rows form the moss st and cable patts and are repeated as required.

Cont straight in patts as set until back measures 38(42:46)cm from cast-on edge, ending with a WS row

Shape raglan armholes

Keeping patts correct, cast off 4 sts at beg of next 2 rows [57(61:65) sts].
Now dec 1 st at each end of next 4 rows [49(53:57) sts].
Now dec 1 st at beg of every row until 13(15:17) sts remain.
Cast off remaining sts.

FRONT

Work as for back to beg of raglan shapings, ending with a WS row.

Shape raglan armholes

Keeping patts correct, cast off 4 sts at beg of next 2 rows [57(61:65) sts].

Now dec 1 st at each end of next 4 rows [49(53:57) sts].
Now dec 1 st at beg of every row until front measures 10(13:15)cms from beg of raglan shaping, ending with a WS row.

Shape front neck

Next row: work to centre 9 sts, put these on st holder **
Next row: dec 1 st at neck edge on this and alt rows 4 times, AT THE SAME TIME cont to dec at raglan edge on alt rows as set until all sts are worked off. Cast off.
With RS of work facing, rejoin yarn to rem sts and patt to end of row.
Patt 1 row, now work as for first side from ** to end.

SLEEVES (2 alike)

With 5mm needles and C cast on 26(30:34) sts and work in k1 p1 rib for 8cm, inc 5 sts evenly over last row [31(35:39) sts].
Change to 6½mm needles and using C for cable patt and MC for moss st patt, work as follows:
1st row: (RS facing) work 11(13:15) sts in moss st in MC, k9 in C, moss st 11(13:15) in MC.
Cont in patt as now set, working cable and moss st patt as for back, AT THE SAME TIME inc 1 st at each end of 3rd row and then every foll 5th row until 51(57:63) sts are on the needle, working inc sts into the moss st at either side.
Now cont straight in patt until sleeve measures 46(48:50)cm from cast-on edge, ending with WS row.

Shape raglans

Keeping patts correct, cast off 4 sts at beg of next 2 rows [43(49:55) sts].
Now dec 1 st at both ends of next 4 rows.
Now dec 1 st at beg of every row until 12 sts remain.

Shape top

Keeping patts correct, cast off 4 sts at beg of next row, now dec 1 st at both ends of every row until 1 st remains.
Cast off

Work second sleeve to match, but reverse the top shaping.

COLLAR

With 5mm needles and C slip sts from spare needle on front cable and cont in cable patt as set until work measures enough to go all around neck edge, including sleeve tops and tuck behind like a shawl collar. Cast off.

TO MAKE UP

Refer to 'Tips for the Professional Finish'.

1) Weave in all ends.
2) Block and pin and steam.
3) Lay work out flat and set in sleeves with an invisible seam.
4) With an invisible seam sew sleeve and side seams.
5) Slip stitch around collar and slip stitch end to inside of front.

WINTER WHITES

KNITTING STANDARD

Description

Semi-tailored jumper, cuffs, welt and collar in ridge stitch.

Materials

Wendy Dolce Shade White

50% Courtelle, 50% Brinylon 9(10:11:12) × 50 gram balls

Wendy Donna Shade Grey

77% Courtelle, 6% Polyester, 15% Mohair, 2% Brinylon 2(2:2:2) × 50 gram balls

Wendy Seta DK White

48% Viscose, 40% Cotton, 9% Silk, 3% Nylon 2(2:2:2) × 50 gram balls

1 pair each needles sizes 4mm, 3¼mm and 3¾mm

3 buttons, stitch holder, spare needle.

Measurements

To fit bust

| 86cm | 91cm | 96cm | 101cm |

Actual measurements

| 92·5cm | 97·5cm | 102·5cm | 107·5cm |

Length from shoulder

| 44cm | 45cm | 47cm | 48cm |

Sleeve seam (approx)

| 42cm | 43cm | 44cm | 45cm |

Additional abbreviations

MC = Wendy Dolce, A = Wendy Donna; B = Wendy Seta.

Tension

24 sts and 27 rows to 10 cm sq over st st on 4mm needles.

NB This garment is colour blocked (see 'Knitting notes').

BACK

With 3¼mm needles and MC cast on 91(97:103:109) sts and work in ridge pattern as follows:

Row 1: (wrong side facing) Knit
Row 2: Purl
Row 3: Knit
Row 4: Knit
Row 5: Purl
Row 6: Knit

These 6 rows form the ridge pattern and are repeated as required. Continue in pattern as set until 36 rows have been worked.

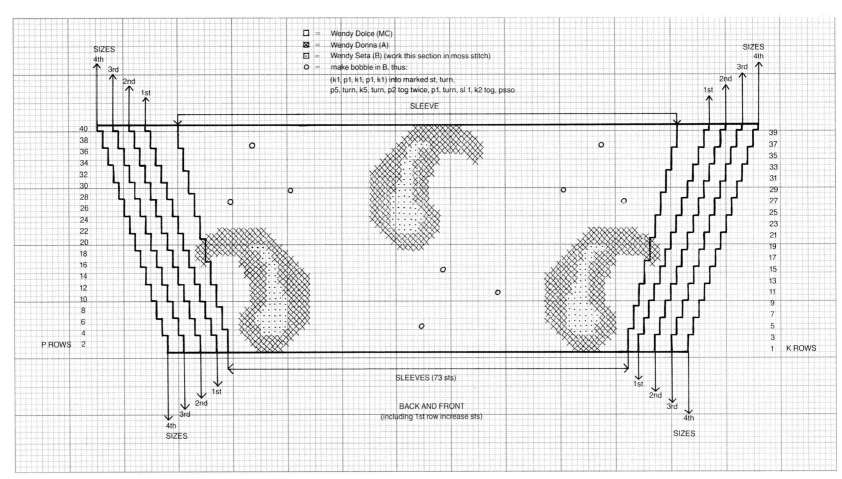

Shape Waist

Keeping pattern correct dec 1 st at each end of next and every foll 8th row until 71(77:83:89) sts remain.

Work 10 rows straight, ending with a wrong side row.

Change to 3¾mm needles and starting with knit row continue in st st, AT THE SAME TIME shape sides by inc 1 st at each end of every foll 3rd row until 75(81:87:93) sts are reached.

Work 2 rows straight, ending with a wrong side row.

Change to 4mm needles and work from chart as follows:

Starting with a knit row work between appropriate lines for the size, and repeat the 40 rows of chart as required, AT THE SAME TIME inc 1 st at both ends of first row and every foll 3rd row as shown, until 111(117:123:129) sts are reached, ending with a wrong side row.

Work 4(6:8:10) rows straight (if necessary, adjust length here).

Shape Armholes

Keeping patt correct, cast off 4 sts at beg of next 4 rows, then dec 1 st at each end of the next 2(2:4:6) rows, work 1 row.

Dec 1 st at each end of next row [87(93:95:97) sts]. **

Continue straight in pattern until back measures 21cm from beg of armhole shaping, ending with a wrong side row.

Shape Shoulders

Cast off 10 sts at beg of next 4 rows, leaving the remaining 47(53:55:57) sts on a stitch holder for back neck.

FRONT

Work as for back to **

Continue straight in pattern until front measures 12cm from beg of armhole shaping, ending with a wrong side row.

Shape Neck

next row: Patt 28(31:32:33) sts and leave these sts on a spare needle.

Patt 31 sts and put these sts onto a st holder, patt to end of row and work on this last set of 28(31:32:33) sts only.

Keeping continuity of pattern dec 1 st at neck edge of every row until 20 sts remain.

Work straight in pattern until front measures same as back at longest point.

Cast off.

With wrong side facing rejoin yarn to sts on spare needle and work to match opposite side.

SLEEVES (2 alike)

With 3¼mm needles and MC cast on 49(53:53:55) sts and work in ridge pattern as for back for 30 rows.

Inc row: (Wrong side facing) p 1(7:7:10), *inc in next st, p1, repeat from * to last 0(6:6:9) sts, p to end [73 sts].

Change to 4mm needles and work from chart as follows:

Starting with a knit row, work between appropriate lines for sleeve, and repeat the 40 rows of chart as required, AT THE SAME TIME shape sides by inc 1 st at each end of every foll 4th row as shown until 117 sts are reached, working the inc sts into the patt.

Continue straight in patt until sleeve measures approx 42(43:44:45)cm from cast-on edge, ending with a wrong side row and on same pattern row as back to start armhole shaping.

Shape Top

Keeping continuity of pattern cast off 4 sts at beg of next 4 rows.

Dec 1 st at each end of the next row and every foll alt row until 59 sts.

Work 1 row.

Cast off 3 sts at beg of next 4 rows.

Cast off remaining 47 sts.

COLLAR

Join right shoulder seam.

With 3¼mm needles and MC, with right side facing, pick up and k 25 sts evenly down front neck edge, k centre 31 sts, pick up and k 25 sts to shoulder seam, k sts of back neck [128(134:136:138) sts].

Repeat rows 1–6 of ridge pattern 6 times, then rows 1–3 again.

Cast off.

BUTTON TAB

With 3¼mm needles and MC cast on 9 sts and work in single rib as follows:

Row 1: (right side facing) k1, * p1, k1, rep from * to end.

Row 2: P1, * k1, p1, repeat from * to end.

Repeat these 2 rows until tab measures 20cm, ending with a 2nd row.

Keeping rib correct dec 1 st at each end of every alt row until 3 sts remain. Sl 1, k2 tog, psso. Fasten off.

SHOULDER PADS (2 alike)

With 3¼mm needles and MC cast on 37 sts. Work in single rib as for button tab until a square is formed.

Cast off loosely in rib.

TO MAKE UP

Check required techniques with
'Tips for the Professional Finish'.

1) Weave in ends.
2) Join shoulder seam.
3) With an invisible seam join collar, sides
   and sleeves.
4) With a fine back stitch set in the sleeves,
   gathering the top to fit the armhole.
5) Sew in shoulder pads.
6) Thread a running stitch down centre of
   front welt, draw up until this measures
   10cm, fasten off.
7) Stitch cast-on edge of tab to last row of welt
   on wrong side. Fold tab over running stitch,
   use the buttons to hold it in place.

'GLOVES'

Materials

Dolce 1 × 50 gram ball

Seta 1 × 50 gram ball

1 pair needles size 3¼mm.

Tension and abbreviations as Sweater.

RIGHT GLOVE

With 3¼mm needles and B cast on 38 sts.
Work 6 rows of ridge patt 5 times (30 rows).
Inc row: P5, *inc in next st, p8; rep from *
ending p5 (42 sts) **

1st row:	with MC k21, p1, k2, p1, k to end.
2nd row:	with MC k1, p to last st, k1.
3rd row:	with MC k21, p1, inc twice in next st, k1, p1, k, to end.
4th row:	as 2nd.
5th row:	with MC k21, p1, k4, p1, k to end.
6th row:	as 2nd.
7th row:	with B k21, p1, (inc in next st, k1) twice, p1, k to end.
8th row:	with B as 2nd.

These 8 rows set stripe patt. Keeping cont of
stripe work as follows:

9th row: k21, p1, k6, p1, k to end.
10th and every foll alt row: as 2nd, using
correct colour.

11th row: k21, p1, inc in next st, k3, k1, inc in
next st, p1, k to end.
Cont in this manner (keeping cont of stripe)
inc 2 sts in thumb gusset on every foll 4th row
until there are 52 sts.
Work 5 rows straight, still working p st either
side of gusset.
Next row: k34, turn.
Foll row: k1, p11, cast on 4 sts, turn [16 sts].
Keeping a k st at each end of every row and
keeping cont of patt, work 18 rows in st st.

Shape Top

1st row: k2 tog to end.
2nd row: k1, p to last st, k1.
Thread yarn through rem sts, fasten off.
With right side facing rejoin yarn, k up 4 sts
from 4 cast-on sts, k18 [44 sts].
Next row: k1, p to last st, k1.
Foll row: k21, k2 tog, k1, k2 tog, k to end
[42 sts].
Work 11 rows.

First Finger

1st row: k27, turn.
2nd row: k1, p11, cast on 3, turn [15 sts].
Work 22 rows on these sts keeping cont of stripe patt and k sts at each end of every row.

Shape Top

1st row: k1, (k2 tog) to end. Complete as thumb.

Second Finger

With right side facing rejoin yarn and k up 3 sts from cast-on sts at base of first finger, k5, turn.
Next row: k1, p12, cast on 2, turn [15 sts].
Work 24 rows as set for first finger.

Shape Top and complete as first finger.

Third Finger

With right side facing rejoin yarn and k up 2 sts from cast-on sts at base of second finger, k5, turn
Next row: k1, p11, cast on 3, turn [15sts].
Complete as first finger.

Fourth Finger

With right side facing rejoin yarn, k up 3 sts from cast-on sts at base of third finger, k5, turn.
Next row: k1, p11, k1, turn [13sts].
Work 18 rows as set for first finger.
Complete as first finger.

LEFT GLOVE

Work as right to **

1st row: with MC, k17, p1, k2, p1, k to end.
2nd row: with MC, k1, p to last st, k1.
3rd row: with MC, k17, p1, inc twice in next st, k1, p1, k to end.
4th row: as 2nd.
5th row: with MC, k17, p1, k4, p1, k to end.
6th row: as 2nd.
7th row: with B, k17, p1 (inc in next st, k1) twice, p1, k to end.
8th row: with B as 2nd.
These 8 rows set stripe patt, keeping cont of stripe work as follows:

9th row: k17, p1, k6, p1, k to end.
10th and every foll alt row: as 2nd using correct colour.
11th row: k17, p1, inc in next st, k3, inc in next st, k1, p1, k to end.
Cont in this manner (keeping cont of stripe) inc 2 sts in thumb gusset on every 4th row until there are 52 sts.
Work 5 rows straight, still working p st each side of gusset.

Next row: k30, cast on 4, turn.
Foll row: k1, p14, k1, turn.
Complete thumb as right glove.
With right side facing k up 4 sts from cast-on sts, k22 [44 sts].
Next row: k1, p to last st, k1.
Foll row: k17, k2 tog, k1, k2 tog, k to end [42 sts].
Work 11 rows straight.

First Finger

Next row: k27, cast on 3, turn.
Foll row: k1, p13, k1.
Complete as first finger on right glove.

Second Finger

With right side facing rejoin yarn, k up 3 cast-on sts at base of first finger, k5, cast on 2, turn.

Next row: k1, p13, k1, turn.
Complete second finger as right glove.

Third Finger

With right side facing rejoin yarn and k up 2 sts from cast-on sts at base of second finger, k5, cast on 3, turn.
Next row: k1, p13, k1.
Complete as third finger on right glove.

Fourth Finger

As right glove.

TO MAKE UP

1) Weave in all ends.
2) With an invisible seam join each finger and side edge.

WINTER WHITES

'DISCOVERY' – Erika

Description

Blouson-style sweater, worked in Aran patterns with contrast colour inserts and rib-pattern pockets and collar details.

Materials

A – *Samband Icelandic Lopi – Aran* 17(18:19) × 50 gram balls

B – *Samband Icelandic Lopi – Grey* 6(6:6) × 50 gram balls

One pair each needles sizes 5½mm (long) and 5mm and a cable needle

Measurements

To fit chest
92cm–97cm   97cm–102cm   102cm–107cm

Actual measurements
117cm   122cm   127cm

Length
66cm   69cm   71cm

Sleeve seam
48cm   51cm   53cm

Tension

14 sts and 21 rows to 10cm sq measured over st st on 5½mm needles.

21 sts and 21 rows to 10cm sq measured over Aran patt and Bobble patt on 5½ needles.

PATTERNS USED

1) DOUBLE ZIG ZAG PATTERN (worked over 20 sts)

1st row: (RS facing) p8, k4, p8
2nd row: and all alt rows: k the p sts and p the k sts of previous row (when the zig zag is worked on the wrong side, k instead of p on each side of crossed sts) and work in moss st inside crossed sts
3rd row: P7, cross 2R (slip 1 st onto cable needle and hold at back of work, k next 2 sts, then k the st from cable needle), cross 2L (slip 2 sts onto cable needle and hold at front of work, p next st, then k the 2 sts from cable needle), p7
5th row: P6, Cr2R, (p1, k1) Cr2L, p6
7th row: P5, Cr2R, (p1, k1) twice, Cr2L, p5
9th row: P4, Cr2R, (p1, k1) 3 times, Cr2L, p4
11th row: P3, Cr2R, (p1, k1) 4 times, Cr2L, p3
13th row: P2, Cr2R, (p1, k1) 5 times, Cr2L, p2
15th row: P2, Cr2L, (p1, k1) 5 times, Cr3 2R, p2

17th row: P3, Cr2L, (p1, k1) 4 times, Cr2R, p3
19th row: P4, Cr2L, (p1, k1) 3 times, Cr2R, p4
21st row: P5, Cr2L, (p1, k1) twice, Cr2R, p5
23rd row: P6, Cr2L, (p1, k1) Cr2R, p6
25th row: P7, Cr2L, Cr2R, p7

Repeat rows 3–26 inclusive to form the centre panel pattern.

2) DIAGONAL PATTERN

K3 sts in st st increasing 1 st on rows where indicated on purl st immediately inside this 3 st edge.

3) CROSS STITCH RIB (worked over 2 sts)

1st row: (RS facing) pass needle in front of first st, k 2nd st, then k first st, slip sts off needle together.
2nd row: P2
Repeat these 2 rows as required.

4) FANCY CABLE (worked over 8 sts)

1st and 5th rows: (RS facing) K8
2nd and all alt rows: P8
3rd row: Slip 2 sts onto a cable needle and leave at front of work, k2, then k2 sts from cable needle, slip 2 sts onto cable needle and leave at back of work, k2, then k2 sts from cable needle.
7th row: Slip 2 sts onto cable needle and leave at back of work, k2 then k2 sts from cable needle, slip 2 sts onto a cable needle and leave at front of work, k2, then k2 sts from cable needle.
8th row: As 2nd row
Repeat these 8 rows as required.

5) BOBBLE STITCH (worked on multiples of 4 sts)

1st row: (RS facing) P.
2nd row: * (k1, p1, k1) into 1st st, p3 tog.
3rd row: P.
4th row: * P3 tog, (k1, p1, k1) into next st.
Repeat these 4 rows as required.

6) REVERSED ST ST AND ST ST RIB (used on pockets and collar)

1st row: P.
2nd row: K.
3rd–4th rows: As 1st and 2nd rows.
5th row: K.
6th row: P.
7th–8th rows: As 5th and 6th rows.
Repeat these 8 rows as required where indicated.

KNITTING STANDARD ✕✕

SLEEVES (2 alike)

When knitting contrast colour use a separate ball of yarn for each colour change, twisting yarn at back of work to avoid a hole. Do not carry yarn along back of work. Refer to 'Knitting Notes' on working in colours.
With 5mm needles and A, cast on 44(48:52) sts and work in k1 p1 rib for 8cm, on last row inc 8(10:12) sts evenly across row [52(58:64) sts].

Change to 5½mm needles and place pattern as follows:

1st row: (RS facing) k3(4:5) B, k3 A, p40(44:48) A, k3 A, k3(4:5) B.
2nd row: P3(4:5) B, p3 A, *(k1, p1, k1) into next st, p3 tog 10(11:12) times, p3 A, p3(4:5) B.
3rd row: As 1st row
4th row: P3(4:5) B, p3 A, * p3 tog, (k1, p1, k1) into next st 10(11:12) times, p3 A, p3(4:5).

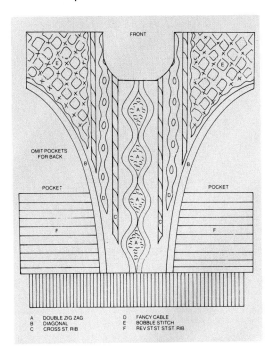

OMIT POCKETS FOR BACK

FRONT

POCKET   POCKET

A	DOUBLE ZIG ZAG	D	FANCY CABLE
B	DIAGONAL	E	BOBBLE STITCH
C	CROSS ST. RIB	F	REV ST ST STST RIB

Repeat pattern as now set, AT THE SAME TIME inc 1 st at each end of every 5th row until 86(92:98) sts are on the needle, working inc sts in B.

Now cont straight in patt as set until sleeve measures 48(51:53)cm from cast-on edge, ending with a WS row.

Cast off all sts.

FRONT

With 5mm needles and A, cast on 84(88:92) sts and work in k1 p1 rib for 7(7:9)cm, on last row inc 12(14:16) sts evenly across row [96(102:108) sts].

Change to 5½mm needles and work in pattern as follows:

1st row: (RS facing) p35(38:41), k3, (p8, k4, p8) of 1st row of zig zag pattern, k3, p35(38:41).

2nd row: K35(38:41), p3, (k8, p4, k8) of 2nd row of zig zag pattern, p3, k35(38:41).

3rd row: P35(38:41), k3, work 3rd row of zig zag pattern, k3, p35(38:41).

4th row: K35(38:41), p3, work 4th row of zig zag pattern, p3, k35(38:41).

The stitches are now set for side pockets in patt no. 6 and centre 20 sts for patt no. 1.

5th row: K34(37:40), slip next st onto cable needle and hold at back of work, k3, p st from cable needle, patt 20 sts of 5th row of zig zag pattern, slip next 3 sts onto cable needle and hold at front of work, p1 st, k3 sts from cable needle, k34(37:40).

6th row: P34(37:40), p3, k1, work 6th row of zig zag pattern, k1, p3, p34(37:40).

7th row: K34(37:40), k3, p1, work 7th row of zig zag pattern, p1, k3, k34(37:40).

8th row: As 6th row working appropriate row on zig zag pattern.

9th row: P33(36:39), cable 3 right as on 5th row, p1, work 9th row of zig zag pattern, p1, cable 3 left as on 5th row, p33(36:39).

10th row: K33(36:39), p3, k2, work 10th row of zig zag pattern, k2, p3, k33(36:39).

11th row: P33(36:39), k3, p2, work 11th row of zig zag pattern, p2, k3, p33(36:39).

12th row: As 10th row working appropriate row on zig zag pattern.

13th row: K32(35:38), cable 3 right, now work 1st row of cross stitch rib, work 13th row of zig zag pattern, work 1st row of cross stitch rib, cable 3 left, k32(35:38).

14th row: P32(35:38), p3, k1, work 2nd row of cross stitch rib, work 14th row of zig zag pattern, work 2nd row of cross stitch rib, k1, p3, p32(35:38).

15th row: K32(35:38), k3, p1, work 1st row of cross stitch rib pattern, work 15th row of zig zag pattern, work 1st row of cross stitch rib pattern, p1, k3, k32(35:38).

16th row: As 14th row working appropriate row on zig zag pattern.

The cross stitch rib pattern is now set on either side of the centre zig zag pattern. Cont in patt as now set until 33rd row has been worked, moving diagonal over 1st on either side, as before on every 4th row.

33rd row: P27(30:33), cable 3R, p1, k2, p2, work 1st row of cross st pattern, work zig zag pattern, work cross st pattern, p2, k2, p1, cable 3L, p27(30:33).

34th row: K27(30:33), p3, k2, p2, k2, p2, work zig zag pattern, p2, k2, p2, k2, p3, k27(30:33).

35th row: P27(30:33), k3, p2, k2, p2, cross stitch pattern, zig zag pattern, cross stitch pattern, p2, k2, p2, k3, p27(30:33).

36th row: As 34th row working appropriate pattern rows.

37th row: K26(29:32), cable 3R, p1, k2, p2, cross stitch pattern, zig zag pattern, cross stitch pattern, p2, k3, p1, cable 3L, k26(29:32).

38th row: P26(29:32), p3, k2, p3, k2, p2, work zig zag pattern, p2, k2, p3, k2, p3, p26(29:32).

39th row: K26(29:32), k3, p2, k3, p2, cross stitch pattern, zig zag pattern, cross stitch pattern, p2, k3, p2, k3, k26(29:32).

40th row: As 38th row working appropriate pattern.

41st row: Cast off 25(28:31) sts, cable 3R, p1, k4, p2, cross stitch pattern, zig zag pattern, cross stitch pattern, p2, k4, p1, cable 3L, k25(28:31).

42nd row: Cast off 25(28:31) sts, p3, k2, p4, k2, p2, zig zag pattern, p2, k2, p4, k2, p3.

Having cast off pockets you now have 46 sts on needle.
From now on the diagonal on the outsides of work will be achieved by increasing inside the '3 sts' as shown on patt 2.

43rd row: K3, p1, k5, p2, cross stitch pattern, zig zag pattern, cross stitch pattern, p2, k5, p1, k3.

44th row: P3, inc into next st kwise, p5, k2, p2, patt 20 sts zig zag pattern, p2, k2, p5, inc into next st kwise, p3.

45th row: K3, p2, k5, p2, cross stitch pattern, zig zag pattern, cross stitch pattern, p2, k4, p2, k3.

46th row: P3, k2, p5, k2, p2, zig zag pattern, p2, k2, p5, k2, p3.

47th row: K3, inc into next st pwise, k6, p2, cross stitch pattern, zig zag pattern, cross stitch pattern, p2, k6, inc into next st, k3.

48th row: P3, k2, p6, k2, p2, zig zag pattern, p2, k2, p6, k2, p3.

49th row: K3, p1, k7, p2, cross stitch pattern, zig zag pattern, cross stitch pattern, p2, k7, p1, k3.

50th row: P3, inc kwise, p7, k2, p2, zig zag pattern, p2, k2, p7, inc kwise, p3.

51st row: K3, p2, k7, p2, cross stitch pattern, zig zag pattern, cross stitch pattern, p2, k7, p2, k3.

52nd row: P3, inc kwise, p8, k2, p2, patt 20, p2, k2, p8, inc kwise, p3.

53rd row: K3, p2, patt 8 (as 1st row of patt no. 3), p2, cross stitch pattern, zig zag pattern, cross stitch pattern, p2, patt 8, p2, k3.

Pattern 4 is now set on the 8 sts from now on referred to as patt 8

Cont in patts as now set, inc inside the '3 sts' on rows 54 and 56.

58th row: P3, inc kwise, p1, k2, patt 8, k2, p2, patt 20 sts, p2, k2, patt 8, k2, p1, inc kwise, p3.

59th row: K3, p2, k1, p2, patt 8, p2, cross stitch pattern, zig zag pattern, cross stitch pattern, p2, patt 8, p2, k1, p2, k3.

60th row: P3, inc kwise, p2, k2, patt 8, k2, p2, patt 20 sts, p2, k2, patt 8, k2, p2, inc kwise, p3.

61st row: K3, p2, cross stitch pattern, p2, patt 8, cross stitch pattern, patt 20, cross stitch pattern, p2, patt 8, p2, cross stitch pattern, p2, k3.

Cont in patts as now set, inc inside the '3 sts' on rows 62, 64, 66.

67th row: K3, p5 (this is the introduction of patt no. 5), cross stitch 2, p2, patt 8, p2, cross stitch pattern, zig zag pattern, cross stitch pattern, p2, patt 8, p2, cross stitch pattern, p5, k3.

68th row: P3, inc kwise (k1, p1, k1) into next st, p3 tog, p2, k2, patt 8, k2, p2, patt 20 sts, p2, k2, patt 8, k2, p2, p3 tog, (k1, p1, k1) into next st, inc kwise, p3

Cont on these patts as set, inc 1 st at inside of the 3 sts on rows 70, 72, 74, 76, 78, 80, 82 and 84.
Now cont in patts inc each side on every row until you have 120(126:132) sts on the needle.
Cont straight discontinuing the 3 st border and including these sts into the bobble pattern until row 102(106:109).

Shape Neck

1st size only:

103rd row: Patt 37 (patt no. 5), cross stitch pattern, p2, patt 8, p2, cross stitch pattern, cast off centre 20 sts, cross stitch pattern, p2, patt 8, p2, cross stitch pattern, patt 34.

Complete both sides of neck to match.
Dec 1 st at neck edge on rows 104, 105, 106, 107, 108, 109, 111, 113, 115, 117.
Cont straight until row 126 has been worked.
Cast off rem 40 sts.

2nd size only

107th row: Patt 37 (patt no. 5), cross stitch pattern, p2, patt 8, p2, cross stitch pattern, cast off centre 20 sts, cross stitch pattern, p2, patt 8, p2, cross stitch pattern, patt 37.

Complete both sides of neck to match.
Dec 1 st at neck edge on rows 108, 109, 110,
111, 112, 114, 115, 117, 119, 121.
Cont straight until row 130 has been worked.
Cast off rem 43 sts.

3rd size only:

110th row   Patt 40 (patt no. 5), p2, k2, patt 8,
            k2, p2, cast off centre 20 sts, p2
            k2, patt 8, k2, p2, patt 40 sts.

Complete both sides of neck to match
Dec 1 st at neck edge on rows 111, 112, 113,
114, 115, 116, 118, 120, 122, 124.
Cont straight until row 133 has been worked.
Cast off rem 46 sts.

BACK

Work rib and inc row as for front.
Change to 5½mm needles.
1st row: Cast off 35(38:41) sts in rib, k3, p8,
          k4, p8, k3, rib 35(38:41).
2nd row: Cast off 35(38:41) sts in rib, p3, k8,
          p4, k8, p3.
Cont as for front, omitting the pocket
instructions and working the incs inside the
'3 st' border from the start.
Cont as for front omitting the neck shaping
and working straight to the top. Cast off on
row 127(131:134).

COLOUR INSETS (make 4)

NB Remember to reverse the shaping for 2 of
the pieces.
With 5½mm needles and B, cast on 33(36:39)
sts.
Starting with a k row work in st st, keep left
side of work straight, but dec 1 st at right side
on the following rows:
5, 9, 13, 17, 21, 25, 29, 33, 37, 41.
Now dec on rows 47, 53, 59.
Now dec on rows 65, 68, 71, 74.
Now dec on every alt row until 3(6:9) sts
remain.
Now dec on every row 3(6:9) times.
2nd size only: All sts should now be worked
off.
3rd size: Cast off rem 3 sts.

COLLAR

Refer to 'Tips for the Professional Finish'. Join
tog one shoulder seam with an invisible seam,
with A pick up and k 100 sts evenly around
neck edge.
With 5mm needles work 10 bands (40 rows of
patt no. 6).
Cast off.

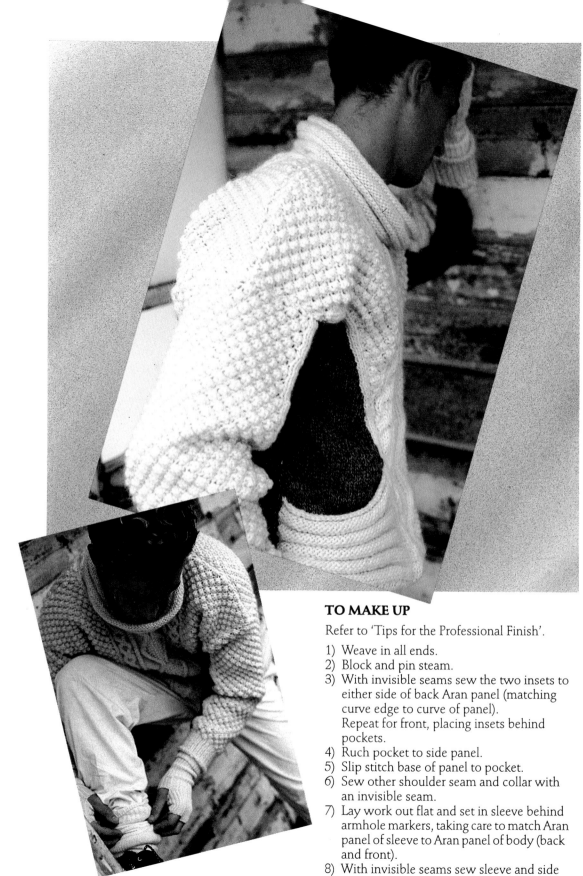

TO MAKE UP

Refer to 'Tips for the Professional Finish'.

1) Weave in all ends.
2) Block and pin steam.
3) With invisible seams sew the two insets to
   either side of back Aran panel (matching
   curve edge to curve of panel).
   Repeat for front, placing insets behind
   pockets.
4) Ruch pocket to side panel.
5) Slip stitch base of panel to pocket.
6) Sew other shoulder seam and collar with
   an invisible seam.
7) Lay work out flat and set in sleeve behind
   armhole markers, taking care to match Aran
   panel of sleeve to Aran panel of body (back
   and front).
8) With invisible seams sew sleeve and side
   seams.

WINTER WHITES

Description

Skirt and top in two versions, one short with collar in 'Fair Isle', the other longer with collar in mock ribs and studs.

Materials

Version 1
Avocet, Alpaca and Mohair 17(18:19:20:21) × 25 gram balls

Avocet Soirée Lurex in Silver Sparkle 1 × 50 gram ball

Version 2
Sunbeam Paris 28(29:30:31:32) × 25 gram balls.

130 silver studs from Creative Beadcraft.

One pair each needles sizes 5½mm and 4½mm.

Measurements

To fit bust

81cm	86cm	91cm	96cm	101cm

Finished measurements

96cm	102cm	108cm	114cm	120cm

Tension

17 sts and 25 rows to 10cm over pattern on size 5½mm needles.

NB When working this pattern do not pull the yarn tight across the back of the slipped stitches as this will affect the tension.

BACK

With 5½mm needles cast on 84(89:94:99:104) sts.
1st row: K1, p1; * p1, yb, sl 3 purlwise, p1; rep from * to last st, k1.
2nd row: (wrong side) k1, p to last st, k1.
These 2 rows form patt.
Cont in patt until work measures 23(24:25:26:27)cm on version 1 or 43(44:45:46:47)cm on version 2.

Shape Armholes while keeping the cont of patt.
Cast off 7 sts at the beg of the next 2 rows [70(75:80:85:90) sts]. **
Cont straight until the back measures 26cm from beg of armhole shaping.
Cast off.

FRONT

Work as back to **
Patt 22(24:26:29:31), leave these sts on a spare needle, cast off 26(27:28:27:28), patt to end of row.
Cont on the last set of 22(24:26:29:31) sts dec 1st at the neck edge of every foll 14th row until 18(20:22:25:27) sts rem.
Work straight until the front matches back. Cast off.
Rejoin the yarn to sts on spare needle, work to match opposite side.

SLEEVES (both alike, all sizes)

With 4½mm needles cast on 54 sts.
Work 15 rows in patt.
Inc row: K1, p4, * inc in next st, p2, rep from * to last 4 sts, p3, k1 [69 sts].
Change to 5½mm needles.
Cont in patt, AT THE SAME TIME shape the sleeve by inc 1 st at each end of every foll 6th row until there are 89 sts on the needles.
Work straight until the sleeve measures 36(38:38:39:39)cm from cast-on edge.
Mark with a contrast thread.
Cont in patt for a further 4.5cm. Cast off loosely.

SHOULDER PADS (make 2)

With 4½mm needles cast on 17 sts.
Work a square in st st. Cast off.

COLLAR

Version 1: With 5½mm needles and Soirée Lurex cast on 126 sts, k3 rows.
Beg with a k row cont in st st foll 29 patt row on chart.
Cont in Soirée. P 1 row, k 3 rows.
K next row to mark the edge, beg with a k row work 4 rows in st st. Cast off loosely.
Fold st st to wrong side, slip stitch into place.

Version 2: With 5½mm needles cast on 27 sts.
1st row: k1, * sl 3 purlwise, yfwd, p2, yb, rep from * to last st, k1.
2nd row: (wrong side) k1, p to last st, k1.
These 2 rows form the patt.
Cont in patt until collar measures 72cm. Cast off.
Attach studs as shown, along p st rows.

TO MAKE UP

Refer to 'Tips for the Professional Finish'.

1) Weave in all ends.
2) With an invisible seam join shoulders, sides and the sleeves to contrast thread.
3) Place rem 4.5cm of sleeve to 7 cast-off sts of back and front, with an invisible seam sew this and rem sleeve edge.
4) With an invisible seam sew collar in place.
5) Sew in shoulder pads.
6) On version 2 attach the rem studs to cuffs.

SKIRT

Materials

Version 1
Avocet, Alpaca and Mohair 13(14:15:16:17) ×
25 gram balls.

Version 2
Sunbeam Paris 23(25:26:27:30) × 25 gram balls.

Elastic 2.5cm wide to fit waist.

Needles and tension as for sweater.

Measurements

To fit hips

| 86cm | 91cm | 96cm | 101cm | 106cm |

Tension As for sweater.

NB Skirt is worked in one piece.

With 5½mm needles cast on
147(152:157:162:167) sts.
1st row: K1, * p1; yb, sl 3 purlwise, yfwd, p1;
rep from * to last st, k1.
2nd row: (wrong side) k1, p to last st, k1.
These 2 rows form patt.
Cont in patt until the skirt measures 21cm.
Cast on 5 sts at the beg of the next 2 rows
[157(162:167:172:177) sts]. **
Cont in patt until the skirt measures
58(59:60:61:62)cm from cast-on edge ending
with a wrong-side row.
Change to 4½mm needles.
Cont in patt until the skirt measures
63(64:65:66:67)cm from cast-on edge ending
with a wrong-side row.
Next row: k1; * p1, k2 tog, k1, p1; rep from *
            to last st k1.
Cont as follows:
1st row: k1; * k1, p2, k1; rep from * to last st,
            k1.
2nd row: k1; * p1, k2, p1; rep from * to last st,
            k1.
These 2 rows form a double rib, cont in rib
until the skirt measures 72(74:75:76:77)cm.
Change to 4mm needles.
Cont in rib for further 5cm. Cast off ribwise.

BACK VENTS (both alike)

With 4½mm needles and right side facing,
pick up and k42 sts evenly along edge. Beg
with 2nd row, work 10 rows in patt. Cast off.

TO MAKE UP

Refer to 'Tips for the Professional Finish'.

1) Weave in all ends.
2) Join centre back seam.
3) With an invisible seam sew 10 rows of vent
   to cast-off sts, place left vent on top, sew
   into place.
4) Make a casing over elastic.

□ = AVOCET ALPACA AND MOHAIR
X = SOIREE LUREX

REPEAT

Description

Waistcoat with tartan or plaid front and diamond-pattern back, featuring three pockets and front points in shiny yarns.

Materials

Penguoin Berlingot

A – Green 7(8:8) × 50 gram balls

B – Blue 5(6:6) × 50 gram balls

C – Purple 1(1:1) × 50 gram ball

One pair each needles sizes 3mm and 3¼mm and spare needles.

5 buttons

Measurements

To fit chest

91–97cm   97–102cm   102–107cm

Actual measurements

102cm   107cm   112cm

Length from shoulder

53cm   56cm   58cm

Tension

24 sts and 24 rows to 10cm sq measured over tartan/plaid pattern on 3¼mm needles.

NB Pattern uses 'stranding or Fair Isle technique' and a chart

BACK

Using 3mm needles and B cast on 121(127:133) sts and work in g st for 7 rows. Change to 3¼mm needles and st st and using 'stranding or Fair Isle technique' place diamonds as follows:

Row 1: k4(7:10) A, * k1 B, k13 A, repeat from * to last 5(8:11) sts, k1 B, k4(7:10) A.

Row 2: p3(6:9) A, * p3 B, p11 A, repeat from * to last 6(9:12) sts, p3 B, p3(6:9) A.

Continue in this manner until 7 sts are worked in diamond in B then decrease diamond back down to 1 st.

Place 2nd set of diamonds as follows:

Row 8: p11(0:3) A, * p1 B, p13 A, repeat from * to last 12(2:4) sts, p1 B, p11(1:3) A.

Continue as before making a diamond in B 7 sts by 7 rows as before.

Repeat this sequence working alternate diamonds every 7 rows until work measures 25cm from cast-on edge.

Shape armholes by casting off 6 sts at beg of next 2 rows.

Dec 1 st at each end of foll 2 rows, then dec 1 st at each end of next 4 alt rows [97(103:109) sts].

Continue straight until work measures 50(53:56)cm from cast-on edge.

Shape shoulders by casting off 9(10:11) sts at beg of next 6 rows.

Work 1 row and cast off remaining 43 sts.

POCKET LININGS (2 and 1)

With A and 3¼mm needles cast on 28 sts and st st for 11cm, leaving sts on a spare needle. Work another pocket lining the same. With A and 3¼mm needles cast on 24 sts and st st for 10cm, leaving sts on a spare needle (for breast pocket).

LEFT FRONT

Using 3¼mm needles cast on 4 sts in A. Whilst referring to chart and following colours as indicated, using 'stranding or Fair Isle technique', make pointed front as follows: Work straight in pattern until 18 rows on all sts have been worked.

Row 19: k20(22:24) in pattern, k28 in B (for pocket top), k18(19:20) in pattern.

Row 20: P18(19:20) in pattern, k28 in B, purl to end in pattern.

Work a further 3 rows with 28 sts garter st for pocket top

Row 24:   P18(19:20), cast off 28 sts in B, p to end in pattern.

Row 25:   K in pattern placing 28 sts from pocket lining in place of those cast off in previous row.

Continue straight until side seam measures 23cm (remember 2cm for band to be added)

Shape armhole by casting off 6 sts at beg of next row, then dec 1 st at armhole edge on next 2 rows, then 1 st at armhole edge on next 4 alt rows.

At the same time work 24 st pocket top in B as before as shown on chart.

When 10 rows have been worked from start of armhole shaping, shape neck by dec 1 st at neck edge on every alt row 16 times, then on every foll 3rd row until 27(30:33) sts remain. Continue straight until work matches back and cast off shoulder to match.

RIGHT FRONT

Work as for left front reversing all shapings and **omitting top pocket.**

Referring to 'Tips for the Professional Finish' with an invisible seam join shoulder seams.

Row 1:   Knit.

Row 2:   Purl.

Row 3:   Cast on 7 sts at beg of row and work in colours as set on chart to last st, inc into last st to m1.

Row 4:   Purl, in patt across all 12 sts.

Rep rows 3 and 4 twice.

Row 9:   Cast on 8 sts at beg of row and work in colours as set on chart to last st, inc into last st to m1.

Row 10:   Purl, in patt across all 37 sts.

Rep rows 9 and 10 once.

Row 13:   Cast on 8(9:10) sts at beg of row and work in colours as on chart to last st, inc into last st to m1.

Row 14:   Purl, in patt across all sts.

Rep rows 13 and 14 once [64(66:68) sts].

Row 17:   Patt 64(66:68) sts, inc into last st to m1

Row 18:   Purl, in patt.

Rep rows 17 and 18 once.

Row 19:   Rep row 17.

Row 20:   Cast on 0(1:2) sts, at beg of row, and purl in patt to end [66(69:72) sts].

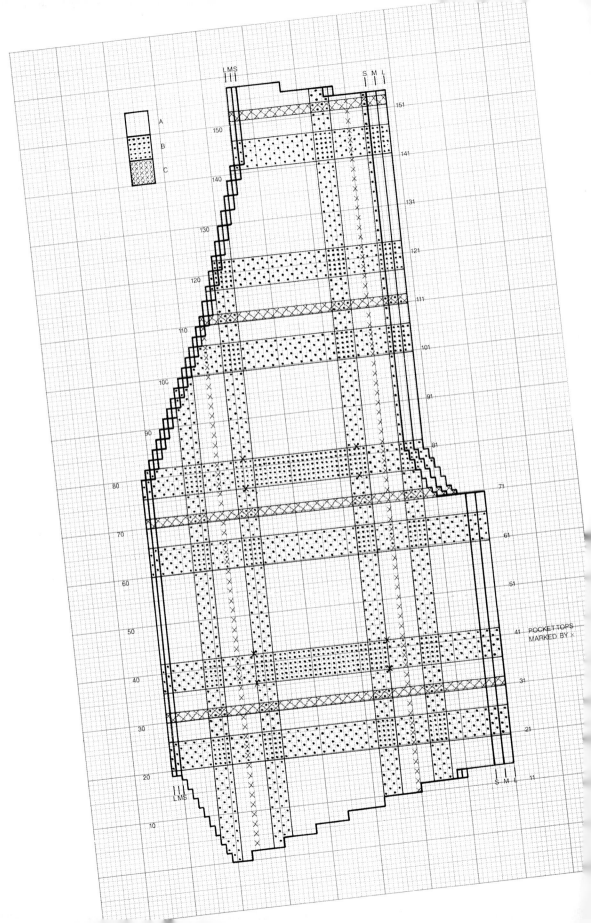

POCKET TOPS MARKED BY X

Garter stitch edgings

These edgings are worked in 4 pieces, each starting from the pointed front of the garment. Make mitre point as follows:
Using 3mm needles and B cast on 1 st.

Row 1: K twice into st.
Row 2: K2.
Row 3: K twice into first st, k1.
Row 4: K3.
Row 5: K twice into first st, k2.
Row 6: K4.
Continue in this manner until 6 sts are reached.
Work straight in g st on these 6 sts until piece is long enough when slightly stretched to go up right front and round neck to centre back of neck (tack as you go). Cast off.
Now work another piece with mitre point to go up left front placing 5 buttonholes as follows:
When piece reaches bottom of front straight edge make a buttonhole by casting off centre 2 sts and casting on over them in next row. Make another 4 buttonholes evenly placed so that 5th buttonhole comes at top of front straight edge. Continue straight to centre back of neck. Cast off.
Make a further 2 pieces to go from mitre point to side edge.

Armhole edges (2)

Using 3mm needles and B cast on 6 sts and work in g st until work is long enough to go round armhole, starting from underarm.

TO MAKE UP

Refer to 'Tips for the Professional Finish'.

1) Weave in all ends.
2) Block and pin and steam.
3) With an invisible seam or slip stitch sew bands all around front edges, taking care to line up 'mitre edges'.
4) Sew armbands into position around armhole edges.
5) Slip stitch pocket linings into position on inside.
6) With an invisible seam sew side seams allowing a 2cm vent at waist edge.
7) Sew on buttons.

Description

Mohair bolero with fuschias and beads.

Materials

George Picaud

MC – Mohair No. 1 9(10:11) × 40 gram balls

– Zig in black 1(1:1:1) × 50 gram ball

– Zig in Fuschia 1(1:1:1) × 50 gram ball

– Feu d'artifice (Lurex) 1(1:1:1) × 20 gram ball

One pair each needles sizes 3¼mm and 4mm, circular needle size 3¼mm 80 cm long

15 bugle beads ref BB15 col 3 from Creative Beadcraft, 15 small gilt beads ref P2½ col 2

Measurements

To fit bust
81–86cm 86–91cm 91–96cm

Actual measurements from cuff to cuff
110cm   113cm   117cm

Length from back neck
53cm   53cm   53cm

Tension

22 sts and 28 rows to 10cm sq measured over st st patt on size 4mm needles.

NB This garment is colour blocked, see 'Knitting Notes'.
JACKET made in one piece.

LEFT FRONT

With 4mm needles, using one end of Lurex and one end of black, cast on 24(26:28) sts. Beg with a k row cont in st st foll patt on chart, at the same time shape side and front edge by inc 1 st at each end of every p row until there are 42(44:46) sts on the needles.
Cont straight at the front edge, but cont to inc side edge until there are 59(61:63) sts on the needles.
Cast on 14(14:15) sts at the beg of the next row. Work 1 row.
Cast on 14(15:16) sts at the beg of the foll row [87(90:94) sts].
Mark with a contrast thread.
Cont in patt for 76 rows.
Inc 1 st at the neck edge of the foll 7 rows.
Leave sts on a spare needle.

RIGHT FRONT

Work as left reversing shaping and patt on chart.

BACK

K sts of left front, while cont to foll chart cast on 33, k sts of right front.
Work 61 rows straight. The chart is now complete. Cont in MC only.
Work 4 more rows.
Mark with a contrast thread.
Cast off 14(15:16) sts at the beg of the foll 2 rows.

Cast off 14(14:15) sts at the beg of the next 2 rows.
Dec 1 st at each end of every P row until 115(119:123) sts rem.
Change to Lurex and black.
K one row, dec as set on P row, k one row.
Leave the rem 113(117:121) sts on a spare needle.

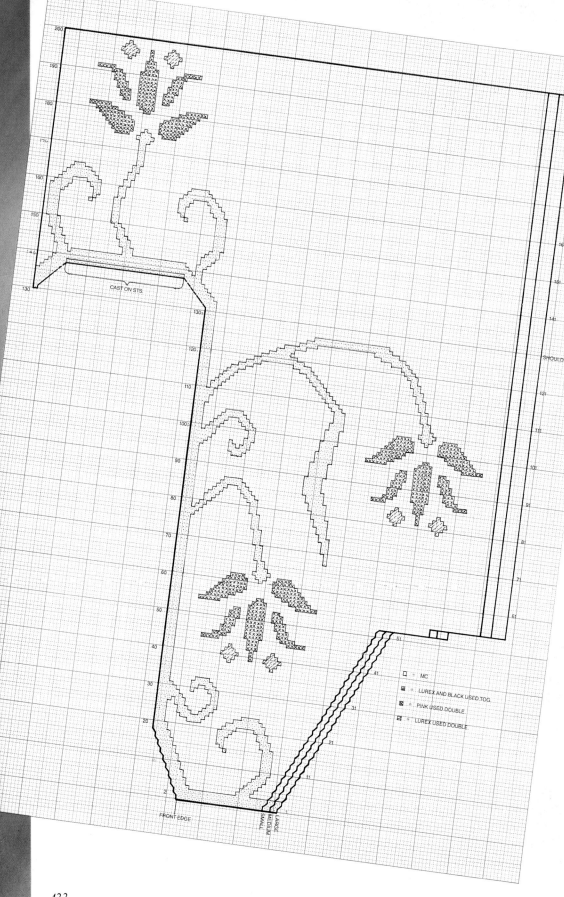

CUFFS (both alike)

With 3¼mm needles and MC and right side facing, pick up and k 138(142:146) sts evenly along edge.
1st row: P2 tog, k2 tog, to the last 2 sts, p2 tog.
2nd row: K1, p1 to last st, k1.
3rd row: P1, k1 to last st, p1.
The 2nd and 3rd rows form rib, rep these 2 rows 7 more times.
Cast off ribwise.

EDGE

First join right side, with an invisible seam. With 3¼mm circular needle and right side facing K sts of back edge, pick up and k23(25:27) sts along cast-on edge, 16 sts up shaped side, 114 sts evenly along edge to cast-on sts of back neck, 31 sts across back neck, 114 sts down edge to beg of shaping, 16 sts along shaped edge and 23(25:27) sts along cast-on edge.
Work 16 rows in k1 p1 rib. Cast off ribwise.

SHOULDER PADS (make 2)

With 3¼mm needles and MC cast on 37 sts. Work a square in k1 p1 rib. Cast off ribwise.

TO COMPLETE

All techniques are listed in 'Tips for the Professional Finish'.

1) Weave in ends.
2) With an invisible seam join left side.
3) Sew on beads as shown.
4) Sew in shoulder pads.

'DELILAH'

KNITTING STANDARD

Description

Skinny rib vest dress with 'keyhole' back.

Materials

Georges Picaud Zig 7(8:9) × 50 gram balls.
Circular needles sizes 3¼mm, 2¾mm and 2¼mm.
One small button.

Measurements

To fit bust
81–86cm   86–91cm   91–96cm

Length from shoulder
75cm   79cm   81cm

Instructions are the same as 'Bali' in Summer.

Description

Loose coat over 'V' back top in diamond checks highlighted with beads.

Materials

Argyll Finesse Mohair

COAT

Main colour 21 × 25 gram balls

Contrast colour 14 × 25 gram balls

One pair each needles sizes 6mm, 5½mm, 5mm and 4½mm.

230 JS12 embroidery stones, from Creative Beadcraft.

TOP

Main colour 10(11:12:12) × 25 gram balls

Contrast colour 9(10:11:11) × 25 gram balls

One pair each needles sizes 6mm and 5½mm.

1 circular needle size 5½mm.

One pair shoulder pads.

Approx 100 JS12 embroidery beads with mounts.

COAT GIVEN IN ONE SIZE ONLY. MEASUREMENTS BELOW REFER TO TOP ONLY.

Measurements

To fit bust

86cm	91cm	96cm	101cm

Actual measurements

96cm	101cm	106cm	111cm

Length from shoulder

68cm	69cm	70cm	71cm

Tension

16 sts and 19 rows to 10cm sq over diamond pattern on 6mm needles.

NB Use Fair Isle technique when working pattern, weaving strands loosely across back of work.

HARLEQUIN COAT

BACK

With 5½mm needles and MC cast on 153 sts and work in single rib as follows:
Row 1: (RS facing) k1, * p1, k1, rep from * to end.

Row 2: P1, * k1, p1, rep from * to end.
Rep these 2 rows twice more.
Change to 6mm needles and starting with a knit row work in st st following patt on chart until back measures 53cm from cast-on edge. Mark each end of last row with a coloured thread.
Cont straight in patt until back measures 84cm from cast-on edge.

Shape Shoulders

Cast off 60 sts, patt 33 sts, cast off remaining 60 sts.
Leave centre 33 sts on stitch holder for back neck.

RIGHT FRONT

With 5½mm needles and MC cast on 83 sts and work 6 rows rib as for back.
Next row: (RS facing) rib 7, and slip these 7

sts onto a safety pin, change to 6mm needles and starting with a knit row work in st st following patt until front measures 53cm from cast-on edge, ending with knit row.
Mark end of last row with a coloured thread.
Continue straight in patt until front measures 74cm from cast-on edge, ending with a purl row.

Shape Front Neck

Next row: Patt 9 sts, and slip these sts onto a safety pin, patt to end.
Keeping patt correct dec 1 st at neck edge on the next 7 rows.

KNITTING STANDARD

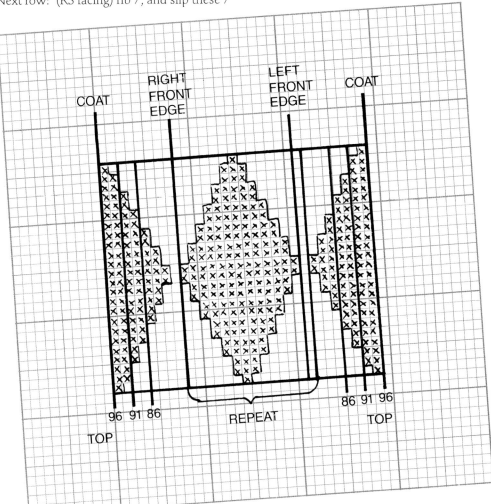

Now work straight in patt on remaining 60 sts until front measures same as back to shoulder, ending with a purl row.
Cast off.

LEFT FRONT

Work as for right front reversing all patterns and shapings.

FRONT BANDS (alike)

Rejoin MC to sts on one safety pin.
With 5½mm needles work in rib as set on bottom welt until band is long enough, when slightly stretched, to go up front to beg of neck shaping.
Leave sts on safety pin.

NECK EDGE

Join both shoulder seams
With 5½mm needles and MC, with right side facing rib 7 sts of right front band, k9 sts from safety pin, pick up and k18 sts to shoulder seam, k33 sts at back of neck, pick up and k18 sts down left front to safety pin, k9 sts from safety pin, rib 7 sts of front band (101 sts)
Work 6 rows in single rib.
Cast off in rib.

CUFFS (alike)

With 5½mm needles and MC, with right side facing, pick up and knit 98 sts evenly between coloured markers.
Next row: (P2 tog, k2 tog) to last 2 sts, p2 tog (49 sts).
Work in single rib for 10cm.
Change to 5mm needles and continue in rib as set until cuff measures 18cm.
Change to 4½mm needles and continue in rib as set until cuff measures 32cm.
Cast off in rib.

TO MAKE UP

Refer to 'Tips for the Professional Finish'.

1) Weave in all ends.
2) Sew on embroidery stones.
3) With an invisible seam sew front bands in place.
4) With an invisible seam join side seams and cuffs.

'HARLEQUIN TOP'

KNITTING STANDARD ✗ ✗ ✗

BACK

With 5½mm needles and MC cast on 77(81:85:89) sts and work in single rib as for coat for 6 rows.

Change to 6mm needles, starting with a knit row work in st st following patt on chart, starting from stitch indicated for size required, repeating the 14 st patt across row and finishing as indicated for size required, rep 24 rows as required until back measures 28cm from cast-on edge, ending with a purl row. **

Shape back neck

Patt 38(40:42:44) sts, leave these sts on a spare needle, patt 1, put this st onto a safety pin, patt to end of row and continue on this last set of 38(40:42:44) sts only.
*** Keeping patt correct dec 1 st at neck edge on next row and every foll 4th row until 21(22:23:24) sts remain.
Work 11(9:7:5) rows straight in pattern. Cast off.
With wrong side facing rejoin yarn to sts on spare needle and work as for first back from *** to end.

FRONT

Work as for back to **
Continue straight in pattern until front measures 60cm from cast-on edge, ending with a purl row.

Shape front neck

Patt 27(29:31:33) sts and leave these sts on a spare needle, patt 23 sts and slip these sts onto a st holder, patt to end of row and continue on these 27(29:31:33) sts only.
*** Keeping patt correct dec 1 st at neck edge on next 6(7:8:9) rows.
Work straight in patt on these 21(22:23:24) sts until front measures same as back to cast-off edge ending with same pattern row. Cast off all sts.
With wrong side facing rejoin yarn to sts on spare needle and work as for first side from *** to end.

NECK EDGE

Join right shoulder seam.
With the circular 5½mm needle, MC and right side facing pick up and k15(17:19:21) sts evenly down left front neck, k across the 23 sts, pick up and k15(17:19:21) sts to shoulder seam, 76(78:80:81) sts down back neck to st on safety pin, k this st (centre back), pick up and k76(78:80:81) sts to open shoulder [206(214:222:228) sts].
Work 6 rows in k1 p1 rib, dec 1 st at either side of centre back st on every row.
Cast off in rib.

ARMHOLE EDGES (alike)

Join remaining shoulder and neck edge seam.
Measure 45 cm up each side from cast-on edge

and mark with a contrast thread.
With 5½mm needles and MC with right side facing, pick up and k85(89:91:95) sts evenly between contrast threads.
Work 6 rows in single rib.
Cast off in rib.

CROSS BACK BANDS

1st Band (top band) With 5½mm needles and MC cast on 3 sts and work in single rib for 26cm. Cast off in rib.

2nd band With 5½mm needles and C cast on 3 sts and work in single rib for 23cm. Cast off in rib.

3rd band With 5½mm needles and MC cast on 3 sts and work in single rib for 20cm. Cast off in rib.

4th band (lower band) With 5½mm needles and C cast on 3 sts and work in single 17cm. Cast off in rib.

TO MAKE UP

Refer to 'Tips for the Professional Finish'.
1) Weave in all ends.
2) Join side seams, matching patterns and using an invisible seam.
   Sew beads onto point of each diamond.
3) Turn armhole edges to the wrong side and slip stitch into place.
4) Place bands as follows: Measure 9cm from shoulder seam down back neck, place 1st band here and sew into place, place 2nd, 3rd and 4th bands 5cm apart.
5) Sew in shoulder pads.

DESIGN NUMBER 33
'MIDNIGHT JACKET' – Erika

Description

Loose-fitting jacket, with waistcoat shaping, rever collar and placket details, using 'colour block' pattern on fronts and back, with Fair Isle technique on sleeves.

Materials

Pinguion

A – Blue/Black Confort DK (used double) 4 × 50 gram balls

B – Orage Mohair Black 6 × 50 gram balls

C – Orage Mohair Pink 2 × 50 gram balls

D – Orage Mohair Blue 4 × 50 gram balls

E – Ruban Pink 1 × 50 gram ball

F – Ruban Turquoise 1 × 50 gram ball

G – Place Vendome Pink, Blue, Silver 1 × 50 gram ball of each used tog as 1 yarn

One pair each needles sizes 4mm and 4½mm

3 Diamante or ornate buttons

Measurements

To fit bust

86cm	92cm	97cm

Actual measurements

104cm	109cm	114cm

Length from shoulder

56cm	58cm	58cm

Sleeve seam

47cm	48cm	50cm

Tension

17sts and 22 rows to 10cm sq over st st on 4½mm needles.

NB This pattern uses colour block method. Refer to 'Knitting Notes'.

BACK

With 4mm needles and A cast on 80(84:88) sts and work in k1 p1 rib for 2½cm.
Change to 4½mm needles and B and st st for 8 rows.

NB! To shape back, whilst following pattern increase 1 st either end of rows 11(12:11), 25(27:25) and 40(43:40).
Row 9: K12(14:16) B, k3 C, k16 B, k6 D (this is the start of the motif for back), k31 B, k3 C, k9(11:13) B.
Continue in st st working centre motif in colours as indicated on graph, and working 3st flashes in C either side, moving these flashes 1 st to the right on every knit row.
Discontinue flashes in C after 10 rows.
Work back in B with just the centre motif, increasing on rows given above.
When last increase is worked mark each end of row with a coloured thread to indicate armhole position.
Continue straight, completing motif and work in B until row 98.
Row 99: (place 3 coloured flashes as follows) K23(25:27) B, k3 D, k19 B, k3 C, k19 B, k3 D, k to end B.
Work flashes for ten rows as before, then continue in B until work measures 53:56:56cm.
Shape shoulders by casting off 9(9:10) sts at beg of next 4 rows, then 10(11:11) sts at beg of next 2 rows. Work 1 row.
Cast off remaining sts.

POCKET LININGS (1 in C, 1 in D)

With 4½mm needles cast on 22 sts and work in st st for 12cm, leave sts on a spare needle.

RIGHT FRONT

With 4½mm needles and D cast on 31(33:35) sts and work in st st as follows:

K4, TURN, slip first st and purl to last st, knit into front and back of last st to make 1.
Next row: K, working a further 4 sts in same way, TURN (i.e. k9 and turn), slip first st, purl to last st and make one.
Work in this way, working an extra 4 sts on k rows and inc 1 st on last st of purl row to make 1 until 25(25:25) sts are being worked.

NB! Start lower motif on 5th row, 7 sts from right (see chart).
Now take 4(4:5) sts into k rows, and inc 1 st on p row until 35(35:35) sts are being worked.
Now take 3(5:6) extra sts into k row and inc 1 st on p row until 39(41:43) sts are reached ***
Continue straight, working colour motif until work measures 10cm from point where 39(41:43)sts were reached.
Increase at side edge to shape front to match back.

Pocket Top

With right side of work facing k8(10:10) sts, k next 22 sts in A, k to end in D.
Work as now set working pocket top in A in k1 p1 rib for 2.5cm, ending with wrong side of work facing.
Next row: p10(10:12) D, cast on 22 in A in rib, p to end in D.
Continue in st st placing pocket lining from spare needle in place of those cast off and starting higher motif 23 sts from front edge (see chart).
Place coloured thread as for back to mark armhole position.

Neck Shaping:

Whilst keeping side straight start neck shaping on rows 22(27:27) from start of higher motif by decreasing as follows:

Dec 1 st at neck edge on next 2 rows, then on alt rows 8 times, every 4th row twice, every 6th row 4 times (16 decreases).
When motif ends work top colours as follows: (count rows from ***)

Row 81: K30(33:35) D

Row 82: P0(0:1) D, 0(2:3) A, 30(31:31) D

Row 83: K29 D, k1(3:5) A

Row 84: P2(4:6) A, 27(28:28) D

Row 85: K26(27:27) D, 3(5:7) A

Row 86: P5(7:9) A, 24(25:25) D

Row 87: K2(2:1) A, 21 D, 7(9:10) A, 0(0:1) B

Row 88: P0(1:3) B, 9(10:10) A, 17 D, 3(4:4) A

Row 89: K5 A, 13 D, 10 A, 1(3:5) B

Row 90: P2(4:6) B, 11 A, 9 D, 6(7:7) A

Row 91: K8(9:9) B, 5 D, 12 A, 3(5:7) B

Row 92: P5(7:9) B, 23(24:24) A

Row 93: K21(22:22) A, 7(9:11) B

Row 94: P9(11:13) B, 17 A, 2(3:3) B

Row 95: K4 B, 13 A, 11(13:15) B

Row 96: P13(15:17) B, 9 A, 5(6:6) B

Row 97: K7(8:8) B, 5 A, 15(17:19) B

Continue in B only until side seam matches
back from above rib and shape shoulders to
match back.

LEFT FRONT

Work as for right front using C as main colour,
reversing all shapings and motifs, and
swapping colours E and F in motifs.
For this front top colour change is as follows:

Row 87: K28(30:32) C, 1(2:2) A

Row 88: P3(4:4) A, 26(28:30) C

Row 89: K24(26:28) C, 5 A

Row 90: P6(7:7) A, 22 C 0(2:0) A, 0(0:2) C

Row 91: K2(4:6) A, 19 C, 7(8:8) A

Row 92: P8(9:9) A, 16 C, 4(6:8) A

Row 93: K5(7:9) A, 14 C, 9(10:10) A

Row 94: P2(3:3) B, 8 A, 12 C,6(8:10) A

Row 95: K7(9:11) A, 10 C, 7 A, 4 B

Row 96: P5(6:6) B, 6 A, 8 C, 7 A, 1(3:5) B

Row 97: K3(5:7) B, 6 A, 6 C, 5 A, 7(8:8) B

Row 98: P8(9:9) B, 6 A, 2 C, 6 A, 5(7:9) B

Row 99: K6(8:10) B, 12 A, 9(10:10) B

Row 100: P10(11:11) B, 10 A, 7(9:11) B

Row 101: K8(10:12) B, 8 A, 11 B

Row 102: P12, B 6 A, 9(11:13) B

Row 103: K1(13:15) B, 2 A, 14 B

Now continue in B only and complete to
match other front.

SLEEVES (2 alike)

With 4mm needles and A cast on 44(48:50) sts
and work in k1 p1 rib for 8cm, increasing
4(4:6) sts evenly over last row [48(52:56) sts].
Change to 4½mm needles and st st and follow
stripe sequence as below whilst increasing
every 4th row until 86(90:94) sts are reached.

Colour B:	12 rows
Colours D and B:	12 rows(i.e. 2 rows D, 1 row seed st, D with B seed st(see diagram) 4 times
Colour B:	22 rows
Colour D:	4 rows
Colour B:	12 rows
Colours D and B:	12 rows seed pattern as before

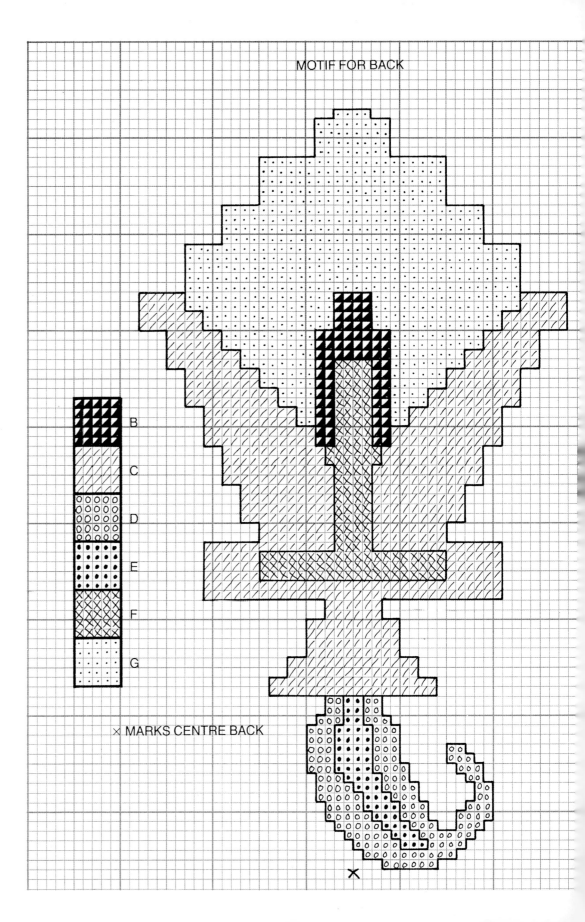

MOTIF FOR BACK

× MARKS CENTRE BACK

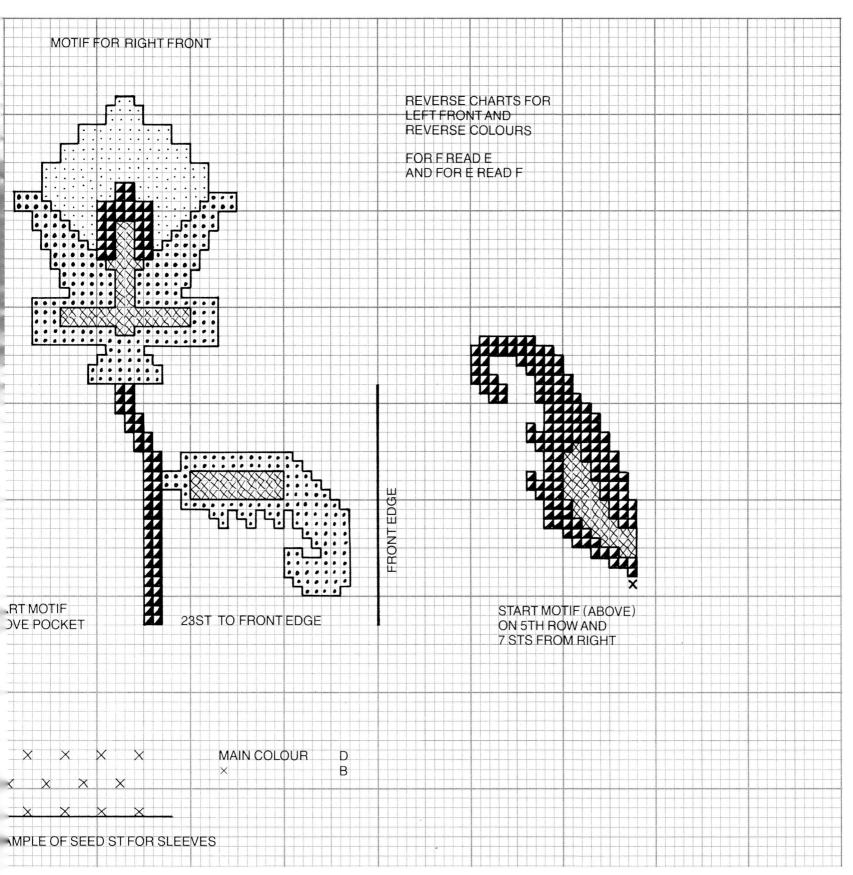

MOTIF FOR RIGHT FRONT

REVERSE CHARTS FOR
LEFT FRONT AND
REVERSE COLOURS

FOR F READ E
AND FOR E READ F

FRONT EDGE

RT MOTIF
VE POCKET

23ST TO FRONT EDGE

START MOTIF (ABOVE)
ON 5TH ROW AND
7 STS FROM RIGHT

× × × ×

MAIN COLOUR   D

×   B

× × × ×

× × × ×

MPLE OF SEED ST FOR SLEEVES

131

Colour B to required length
Continue straight until work measures
47(48:49.5)cm

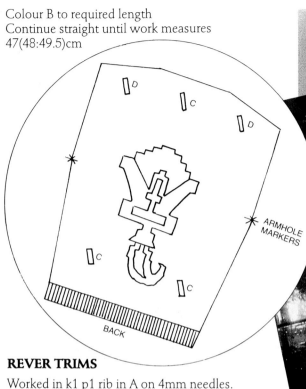

REVER TRIMS

Worked in k1 p1 rib in A on 4mm needles.

Left Front

Cast on 1 st and make mitre point as follows:

Row 1: K into front and back of st to make 1.

Row 2: Rib 2

Row 3: K1, p and k into st to make 1

Row 4: Rib 3

Row 5: K1, p1, k and p into st to make 1

Row 6: Rib 4

Continue in this way until there are 6 sts on needle.

Taking start point from point on front of jacket work in k1 p1 rib until band is long enough to reach neck shaping (when slightly stretched), tack as you go to ensure a good fit.

Now increase at neck edge only to correspond with decreases worked on fronts until 22 sts are reached.

From straight edge cast off 18 sts, rib to end. Next row: Rib 4, cast on 14 sts.

Now work in rib on these 18 sts until work is long enough to go round neck to finish at centre back. Cast off in rib.

Work another piece for right front placing 3 buttonholes (2 sts) evenly spaced up the straight edge of front, complete to meet other piece at back.

Work another 2 pieces, starting with mitre point, long enough to go from point of waistcoat to side edge.

TO MAKE UP

Refer to 'Tips for the Professional Finish'.

1) Weave in all ends.

2) Catch down pocket linings in the correct colour.

3) Lay work out flat and join shoulder seams.

4) Place sleeve tops between markers and sew with an invisible seam.
   Sew sleeve seams and side edges as far as rib.

5) Sew on rever trims neatly making sure buttonholes and shapings are placed in the correct place.

6) Join the collar shapings at back of neck.

7) Sew on trims to side of garment, but leave side vent, do not join front and back ribs.

8) Sew on buttons.

9) Roll back collar and fold back rever above top button.

WINTER NIGHTS

Description

Beaded evening suit with shirt tail, deep 'V' back and lace inset.

Materials

Robin Diamonte DK 87% Acrylic 13% Nylon

Top: 5(5:6:6) × 50 gram balls

Skirt: 8(9:10:11) × 50 gram balls

One pair each needles sizes 4mm and 3¼mm

71 Crystal Drops ref no. MCD col 4 from The Brighton Bead Shop.

1 button to match crystals.

Elastic 2.5cm wide to fit waist.

NB Be sure to knit edge stitches on both knit and purl rows, to make a firm selvedge.

Instructions for skirt are the same as 'Mirage' in Summer.

Measurements

To fit bust

81cm	86cm	91cm	96cm

Actual measurements

92cm	98cm	103cm	109cm

Additional Abbreviation

yrn = yarn round needle.

Tension

22 sts and 28 rows to 10cm sq over st st on size 4mm needles.

BACK

With 4mm needles cast on 6 sts.
K one row.
Beg with a p row cont in st st casting on 3 sts at the beg of every row until there are 102(108:114:120) sts on the needles.
Mark with a contrast thread **
Cont in st st until the back measures 20(21:22:22)cm from contrast thread, ending with a p (WS) row.

Divide and Shape Back

K50(53:56:59), turn, leaving rem sts on a spare needle.
Cont on first sts, work 1 row straight, dec 1 st at the centre back edge of the next row, work 1 row straight.
Rep the last 3 rows 12(13:14:15) more times [37(39:41:43) sts]. Work 0(1:0:1) row.

Shape Armhole

Cast off 3 sts at the beg of the next row, k to end.
Dec 1 st at the beg (centre back) of the next row, p to end.
Cast off 3 sts at the beg of row, k to end.
Work 1 row straight. Dec 1 st at each end of the next row.
Work 1 row straight.
Rep the last 3 rows until 20(22:24:26) sts rem.
Cont working straight at the centre back edge, but cont to shape the armhole edge on every 3rd row until 2 sts rem. Cast off.
Rejoin yarn to sts on spare needle.
K2 tog, put this st on a safety pin, k to end.
Work the rem 50(53:56:59) sts to match the opposite side.

FRONT

With 4mm needles cast on 48 sts.
Work as back to **
Cont in st st until the front measures 24(25:26:26)cm from contrast thread ending with a p row.

Shape Armholes and beg Eyelet patt

1st row:	Cast off 3, k next 45(48:51:54), k2 tog (yrn) twice, sl 1, k1, psso, k49(52:55:58).
2nd row:	Cast off 3, p to end working k1 p1 into all made sts.
3rd row:	Cast off 3, k next 40(43:46:49), (k2 tog, yrn twice, sl 1, k1, psso) twice, k44(47:50:53).
4th row:	as 2nd.
5th row:	K1, k2 tog, k36(39:42:45), (k2 tog, yrn twice, sl 1, k1, psso) 3 times, k36(39:42:45), k2 tog, k1.
6th row:	K1, p to last st, working k1 p1 in all made sts, k last st.
7th row:	K36(39:42:45), (k2 tog, yrn twice, sl 1, k1, psso) 4 times, k36(39:42:45).
8th row:	K1, p2 tog, p to last 3 sts, working k1 p1 in all made sts, p2 tog, k1.
9th row:	K33(36:39:42), (k2 tog, yrn twice, sl.1, k1, psso) 5 times, k33(36:39:42).
10th row:	as 6th.

These rows set patt.
Cont in patt inc no. of sts worked in eyelet lace on every RS row and dec 1 st at each end of every 3rd row until all the sts are incorporated into the eyelet patt.
Cont in patt but cont to dec on every 3rd row (while keeping cont of patt) until 62(64:66:68) sts rem, ending with a WS row.

Shape Neck

While keeping cont of patt, and cont to dec armhole edge on every 3rd row.
Patt 20(21:22:23), turn, leaving the rem sts on a spare needle.
Cont on these 20(21:22:23) sts, dec 1 st at the neck edge of the foll 14(15:15:16) rows [1(1:2:2) sts].
Cast off.
Rejoin yarn to sts on spare needle.
K22, put these sts on to a st holder, patt to end.
Work the rem 20(21:22:23) sts to match the opposite side.

BACK NECK EDGE

With a 3¼mm needle and right side of work facing pick up and k112(116:118:120) sts evenly along right edge, k st on safety pin, pick up and k112(116:118:120) sts evenly along left edge.
Work 6 rows in k1 p1 rib, dec 1 st either side of centre back sts on every row.
Cast off ribwise, dec on this row also.

LOWER BACK EDGE AND FRONT EDGE (Alike)

With 3¼mm needles and right side facing, pick up and k103(109:115:121) sts evenly along edge.
Work 6 rows in rib, dec 1 st at each end of every alt row.

RIGHT ARMHOLE EDGE

With an invisible seam join sides, from underarms down front edge.

With 3¼mm needles cast on 6, with right side of work facing pick up and k57(59:61:63) sts to side seam, 1 st at side seam, 63(65:67:69) sts up back edge [127(131:135:139) sts].
Work 6 rows in rib, dec 1 st either side of side seam st on every alt row.

LEFT ARMHOLE EDGE

With 3¼mm needles and right side of work facing, pick up and k63(65:67:69) sts down back edge to side seam, 1 st at seam, 57(59:61:63) sts up front edge, cast on 6 [127(131:135:139) sts].
Work as right armhole edge.

NECK EDGE

With an invisible seam join both armhole edges at shoulders.
With 3¼mm needles cast on 27 sts, with right side of work facing, pick up and k5 sts across left back neck edge, 1 st at cast-off sts, 5 sts down cast-on sts of armhole, 14 sts to sts on st holder, k10, k2 tog, k10, 14 sts up right neck edge, 5 sts up cast-on sts of armhole, 1 st at cast-off sts, 5 sts across back neck edge, cast on 27.
Work 2 rows in rib.

Buttonhole

1st row: rib to last 6 sts, cast off 2, rib to end.
2nd row: rib 4, cast on 2, rib to end.
Work 2 more rows in rib.
Cast off ribwise loosely.

TO COMPLETE

All the techniques are given in 'Tips for the Professional Finish'.

1) Weave in all ends.
2) Sew on button.
3) Sew 17 beads evenly spaced down back neck edge, 9 beads along lower back edge and 7 along front edge.
4) Sew 9 beads evenly spaced along edge of lace inset, then the remaining beads at random over lace.

Description

Turtle-neck sweater with drop shoulders, worked in 'scroll pattern', with contrast diamond-patterned band details, and 'V' neck 'scroll pattern' cardigan.

Materials

Scroll Sweater

Rowan Fine Chenille

MC – Fuschia 400(400:450) grams

C – Black 200(200:250) grams

Scroll Cardigan

Rowan Fine Chenille

MC – Turquoise 450(450:500) grams

C – Black 250(250:300) grams

One pair each needles sizes 3¾mm, 3mm (long) and 2¾mm (long) and stitch holder.

3 ornate buttons for cardigan

Measurements

To fit bust/chest
86–91cm   97–101cm   107–112cm

Actual measurements
117cm   122cm   127cm

Length from shoulder
69cm   71cm   74cm

Sleeve seam
48cm   51cm   53cm

Tension

24 sts and 24 rows to 10cm sq measured over scroll pattern on 3¾mm needles.

NB Pattern uses 'stranding or Fair Isle technique' throughout and is worked from a chart.

BACK (for both sweater and cardigan)

With 2¾mm needles and C cast on 128(134:140) sts and work in st st for 8 cm, ending with a knit row.
Knit 1 row (to form ridge row for fold).
Change to 3mm needles but continue in st st using C and MC, working diamond pattern for border for 8 cm, referring to chart.

Inc row: (last row of border), p5(8:11), * inc into next st, p12, rep from * to last 6(9:12) sts, inc into next st, purl to end [138(144:150) sts].

Change to 3¾mm needles and continue in st st working 'scroll pattern' from chart using 'stranding or Fair Isle technique'.

When work measures 39(41:42) cm from ridge row place a coloured thread at each end of next row to indicate armhole position. ***
Continue straight until work measures 66(69:71) cm from ridge row.

Shape shoulders

Cast off 15(16:17) sts at beg of next 2 rows, then 16(16:17) sts at beg of next 2 rows, then 16(17:17) sts at beg of foll 2 rows.

Work 1 row and cast off remaining 44(46:48) sts.

SLEEVES (for both sweater and cardigan)

With 2¾mm needles and C cast on 60(62:66) sts and work in st st for 8 cm, ending with a knit row. Knit 1 row to form a ridge row for fold.

Change to 3mm needles and using C and MC work diamond pattern for cuff for 8 cm, referring to chart for sleeve.

Inc row: P4(5:7), * inc into next st, p10, rep from * to last 5(6:8) sts, inc into next st, purl to end [66(68:72) sts].

Change to 3¾mm needles and work 'scroll pattern' as given on chart for sleeve on row 31 (above diamond pattern), AT THE SAME TIME inc 1 st at each end of every 3rd row until 128(134:140) sts are reached.

Continue straight until work measures 48(51:53) cm. Cast off.

Work another sleeve alike.

THE FRONT (for sweater only)

Work as for the back to ***
Continue straight until work measures 60(62:65) cm, ending with right side facing.

Shape neck

Whilst continuing in 'scroll pattern' k54(56:58), place centre 20(22:24) sts on a stitch holder, k to end.

Work on each side of front individually as follows:

Cast off 2 sts at neck edge on next row, then dec 1 st at neck edge on every row until 48(50:52) sts remain.

Work 1 row then dec 1 st at neck edge on next row, [47(49:51) sts].

Work straight until front is same length as back and cast off shoulders to match shoulder shaping for back.

COLLAR (sweater only)

Refer to 'Tips for the Professional Finish' and join one shoulder seam with an invisible seam.

With C and 3mm needles pick up 16(17:18) sts down side of neck, 20(22:24) sts from holder at front, 16(17:18) sts up other side of neck and 44(46:48) sts from back [96(102:108) sts].

Work 3 sets of diamonds in C and MC as for borders.

Work 1 ridge row.

Change to MC and work in st st for 8cm. Cast off.

Sew other shoulder seam with an invisible seam.

'SCROLL CARDIGAN'

FRONTS (for cardigan only)

Pocket linings (2 alike)

With 3¾mm and MC cast on 33 sts and work in pattern from section of chart marked for pocket linings for 15 cm, leaving sts on a spare needle.

RIGHT FRONT

With 2¾mm needles and C cast on 57(60:63) sts and work in st st for 8 cm.
Knit 1 row to form ridge as for back.
Change to 3mm needles and using C and MC work diamond pattern for 8cm, referring to chart.

Inc row: P6(7:8), * inc into next st, p10, rep from * to last 7(9:11) sts, inc into next st, purl to end [62(65:68) sts].
Change to 3¾mm needles and work 'scroll pattern' from chart.
When work measures 19cm from 'ridge row' work pocket top (to match borders) as follows:
With right side facing knit 12 in 'scroll pattern', k33 in diamond pattern (refer to pocket top detail on chart), k17(20:23) sts in 'scroll pattern'.
Continue working like this until pocket top has been worked for 9 rows.
Next row: P17(20:23) in 'scroll pattern', cast off 33 sts firmly, p12 in 'scroll pattern'.
Now continue in 'scroll pattern' placing stitches from pocket lining in place of those sts cast off in previous row.
Continue in pattern until work measures 37 cm, then shape neck as follows:
Whilst keeping to 'scroll pattern' dec 1 st at neck edge on next 3 rows, then dec 1 st at neck edge on next 5 alt rows, then on every foll 4th row 4 times, then every foll 6th rows until 47(49:51) sts remain.
Continue straight until the front is the same length as the back and cast off shoulder to match as for one side of back.

LEFT FRONT

Work as for right front, reversing shapings and following chart for left front.

BUTTONHOLE BAND

Referring to 'Tips for the Professional Finish' join shoulder seams with an invisible seam.
Using 3mm needles and starting at bottom of right front edge for woman and left for man,

pick up 134(140:146) sts up front, then pick up 22(23:24) sts from back of neck (ending at centre back) [156(163:170) sts].
Using C and MC work in diamond pattern as for cuff for 3cm.

Next row: Place 3 buttonholes as follows from bottom of front, pattern 14 sts, cast off next 3 sts, * patt 42 sts, cast off 3 sts, rep from * once.
Continue in pattern to end of row.

Next row: Work in patt casting on 3 sts over those cast off in previous row.

Continue until work measures 6cm, work 1 ridge row.
Continue to work in C only and st st but change to 2¾mm needles and work 3 buttonholes to correspond when facing is folded over.
Cast off.

BUTTON BAND

Work as for the buttonhole band omitting the buttonholes

TO MAKE UP

Refer to 'Tips for the Professional Finish'.

1) Weave in all ends.
2) Block and pin and steam.
3) Lay work out flat and with an invisible seam set in sleeves between armhole markers.
4) With an invisible seam sew sleeve seams.
5) With an invisible seam sew side seams.
6) Join collar seam with an invisible stitch.
7) Turn work to inside and fold all facings to inside and slip stitch into position.
8) For cardigan only – slip stitch pocket linings into position.
9) For cardigan only – sew on buttons and slip stitch around button holes.

"If Winter comes, can Spring be far behind?"

Percy Bysshe Shelley

ACKNOWLEDGEMENTS

Photography	**MICHAEL WOOLLEY**
Michael Woolley's assistant	LAUREN HICKS
Design Concept and Art Direction	IAN HARRIS
Design and Artwork	BOB SAMPSON
Illustrations	HILARY KIDD
Typesetting in Stempel Schneidler	FORCE 9
Technical Illustrations	IAN HARRIS
Pattern Checkers	INESE I AIVARS TINA EGLETON ANNE MATTHEWS *at Vogue* MARILYN WILSON

SPRING *Shot on location at Tunbridge School for Boys, Kent*

Models	KATHY COULTER *at Models 1* MICHAEL THOMPSON *at Models 1*
Stylist	ANNE DRUMMOND
Hair and Make-up	FIONA MOORE *at Models 1*
Clothes	MARKOS ALEXANDER
Shoes	HOBBS
Hats	THE HAT SHOP: *Covent Garden*

SUMMER *Shot at Studio Worx, London*

Models	JOANNA STYBURSKA *at Models 1* MICHAEL THOMPSON *at Models 1*
Stylist	SUSI HORNUNG
Hair	DEBBIE HORGAN
Make Up	FIONA MOORE *at Models 1*
Clothes and Fabric	LIBERTY
Shoes	THE NATURAL SHOE STORE, *London*

AUTUMN   *Shot on location in the Itchen Valley, Hampshire*

Models	KATHY COULTER *at Models 1* RON DWYER *at Laraine Ashton*
Stylist	SUSI HORNUNG
Hair and Make-up	FIONA MOORE *at Models 1*
Clothes	MOLTO! NIGEL PRESTON ELAINE CHALLONER
Hats	GABRIELLA LIGENZA
Shoes	TRICKER AND GRENSON *at Berk* THE NATURAL SHOE STORE, *London*

WINTER   *Shot on location on The West Pier, Brighton and at Leighton House, London*

WINTER WHITES

Models	ALEXANDRA *at Syncro* IAN ANDERSON *at Laraine Ashton*
Stylist	JUDY RUMBOLD
Hair	DEBBIE HORGAN
Make-up	FIONA MOORE *at Models 1*
Clothes	MOLTO! JOSEPH
Shoes	DR MARTEN CHARLES JOURDAN
Hats	FRED BARE

WINTER NIGHTS

Models	ROBERT ABERNETHY *at Select* CECILIA RAE *at Premier* SARAH BRUMM *at Models 1*
Stylist	JOY ANDREWS
Hair and Make-up	FIONA MOORE *at Models 1*
Clothes	AZZEDINE ALAÏA CHARLIE ALLEN
Shoes	MAUDE FRIZON

And of course special thanks to all our wonderful knitters.

STOCKISTS AND DISTRIBUTORS

Addresses to contact for information on stockists and mail order of the yarns and materials used in this book.

United Kingdom

Argyll Wools Ltd
P.O. Box 15
Priestley Mills
Pudsey
West Yorkshire LS28 9LT.

Avocet
Hammertain House
Hookstone Avenue
Harrogate
West Yorkshire HG2 8ER.

Forsell
T. Forsell & Son Ltd
Blaby Road
S Wigston, Leicester

Georges Picaud
Priory Yarns
24 Prospect Road
Osset
West Yorks WF5 8EA.

Hayfield Textiles Ltd
Glusburn
Keighley
West Yorkshire BD20 8QP.

Jaeger Handknitting Yarns
Kilncraig Mills
Alloa
Clackmannanshire
Scotland FK10 1EG.

Kilcara Yarns
Unit 3
Spur Mill
Broadstone Hall Road South
Reddish
Stockport
Cheshire.

Knitting Fever
Smallwares Ltd
17 Galena Road (King St.)
Hammersmith
London W6 0LU

North America

Argyll Wools Ltd
Estelle Designs & Sales Ltd
1135 Queen Street East
Toronto
Ontario
Canada M4 M1 K9

Avocet
Beth Importers Ltd
4675 Pickering Road
Birmingham
Michigan 48010
U.S.A

Forsell
Write to T. Forsell & Son Ltd
Blaby Road
S Wigston, Leicester

Georges Picaud
Merino Wool Co. Inc.
230 Fifth Avenue
Suite 2000
New York 10001
U.S.A

Hayfield Textiles Ltd
Sheepherd Wools Inc.
711 Johnson Avenue
Blaine
Washington 98230
U.S.A

Jaeger Handknitting Yarns
Distributed by Susan Bates
Rte 9A
Chester, CT 06412
U.S.A.

Kilcara Yarns
Reynolds Ltd
15 Oser Avenue
Hayppauge
New York 11788
U.S.A.

Knitting Fever
180 Babylon Turnpike
Roosevelt
New York 11575
U.S.A

United Kingdom

Lister Lee
George Lee & Sons Ltd
P.O. Box 37
Wakefield
West Yorkshire

Neveda Yarns (Amber Yarns)
Greendale Mills
Thackley Old Road
Windhill, Shipley
W. Yorks. BD18 1QB

Offray Ribbon
C.M. Offray & Sons Ltd.
Fir Treet Place
Church Road
Ashford
Middlesex

Patons
Paton & Baldwins Ltd
McMullen Road
Darlington
Co. Durham DL1 1YH

Pingouin
French Wools Ltd
7-11 Lexington Street
London W1

Richard Poppleton
Albert Mill
Horbury
Wakefield
West Yorkshire.

Robin Wools Ltd
Robin Mills
Idle
Bradford
West Yorkshire.

Rowan Yarns
Green Lane Mill
Washpit
Holmfirth
Huddersfield
West Yorkshire HD7 1RW.

North America

Lister Lee
Yarns Plus
120-5726 Burleigh Crescent
Calgary
Alberta
Canada T2H 128

Neveda Yarn Co.
199 Trade Zone Drive
Ronkonkoma
N.Y. 11779
U.S.A

Offray Ribbon
4060 St. Catherine Street West
Suite 720
Westmount
Montreal P.Q. H322X7
Canada.

Patons
Distributed by Susan Bates
Rte 9A
Chester, CT 06412
U.S.A.

Pingouin
Promafil Corpn. (USA)
9179 Red Brandon Road
Columbia
Maryland 21045
U.S.A

Richard Poppleton
White Buffalo Mills Ltd.
6365 Kestrel Road
Mississauga
Ontario L5T 1S4
Canada

Robin Wool
Plymouth Yarn Co. Inc.
500 Lafayette Street
Bristol
PA 19007
U.S.A

Rowan Yarns
Westminster Trading Corporation
5 Northern Boulevarde
Amherst
New Hampshire 03031
USA

Samband
Viking Wools
Rothay Holme
Ambleside
Cumbria

Schachenmayr Nomotta
Aero Needles Group Ltd.
Box No. 2
Edward Street
Redditch
Worcs. B97 6HB

Schaffhauser
Smallwares Ltd
17 Galena Road (King St.)
Hammersmith
London W6 0LU

Scheepjeswool U.K. Ltd
7 Cole Meadow Road
North Moons Moat
Redditch
Worcs. B98 9NZ

Sunbeam Knitting Wools
Crawshaw Mills
Pudsey
Yorkshire.

Twilleys
Roman Mill
Stamford
Lincs.

Tootal Knit Yarns
Tootal Craft Ltd.
56 Oxford Street
Manchester M60 1HJ

Wendy Wools
Carter & Parker Ltd.
Guiseley
West Yorkshire LS20 9PD

Samband
Brookman & Sons Inc.
4416 North East 11th Avenue
334 Fort Lauderdale
Florida 33 334
U.S.A

Schachenmayr Nomotta
Leisure Arts Inc.
P.O. Box 5595
Little Rock
Arkansas 72215
U.S.A

Schaffhauser
Qualitat Ltd
3489 NW Yeon
Portland
Oregon 97210
U.S.A.

Scheepjeswool USA Inc.
155 Lafayette Avenue
N. White Plains
N.Y. 10603
U.S.A

Sunbeam Wools
Estelle Design & Sales Ltd.
1135 Queen Street East
Toronto
Ontario
Canada M4 M1 K9.

Twilleys
Rainbow Gallery
13615 Victory Boulevard
Suite 245
Van News
California 91401
U.S.A

Tootal Knit Yarns
Write to Tootal Craft Ltd. in England.

Wendy Wools
White Buffalo Inc.
Suite 211
Peace Bridge Plaza WHSE
Buffalo
NY 14213
U.S.A

Brighton Bead Shop
Sydney Street
Brighton
Sussex
England

Creative Beadcraft Ltd.
Unit 26
Chiltern Trading Estate
Earl Howe Road
Holmer Green
High Wycombe
Bucks
England.

Jason
Jason Works
Wanless Road
London SE24 0HP

Liberty
Regent Street
London W1.